8-18-66

THE
ACT
OF
BECOMING

THE
ACT
OF
BECOMING

ROBERT W. HITES

ABINGDON PRESS

NEW YORK • NASHVILLE

THE ACT OF BECOMING

Copyright © 1965 by Abingdon Press

All rights in this book are reserved.
No part of the book may be reproduced in any
manner whatsoever without written permission of
the publishers except brief quotations embodied in
critical articles or reviews. For information address
Abingdon Press, Nashville, Tennessee

Library of Congress Catalog Card Number: 65-20369

SET UP, PRINTED, AND BOUND BY THE
PARTHENON PRESS, AT NASHVILLE,
TENNESSEE, UNITED STATES OF AMERICA

TO   1374484
MY
WIFE
MARGARET ANN

FOREWORD

No book has its beginning at a particular point in time. In a sense, a book reflects the life history of an individual. It is the result of intimate life in the family, dialogues extending over the years with friends, teachers who have struck a meaningful chord, books one has studied carefully, and books one has perused casually. There are individuals who have influenced the course of one's life more than others. It is to these I must offer gratitude for their influence.

To my parents I owe not only a Christian rearing but also an abiding interest in and curiosity about people. Robert Price was my minister when I was a young man; his counsel influenced me to prepare for Christian service. It was in discussion with Arthur V. Thurman, another Methodist minister, that I began to see the relevance of what I had learned in graduate studies in psychology to the problems of living as a Christian in our contemporary world. John Perkins, pastor of McCoy Methodist Church, Birmingham, Alabama, has listened to me patiently and has read the manuscript with tolerance. I am grateful to Dr. J. Ralph Jolly, president of Greensboro College, who first read my manuscript and offered encouragement.

And last are those who endured the preparation of the manuscript. My two sons, Robert and Thomas, postponed many outings so that "the book" could be finished. My wife, Margaret Ann, edited copy, typed the final manuscript, and gave constant encouragement.

Robert W. Hites
Greensboro College

CONTENTS

INTRODUCTION

The worker in the church is expected to use many of the methods of modern psychology without being provided an explanation as to why these methods are better than other methods. Much of the church literature which is provided for the church worker asks him to consider the needs of the student and to use methods of group work throughout his teaching. It is the purpose of this book to give some background knowledge of the development of needs, self, attitudes, motives, values, goals, and the effect of groups upon these.

Many church workers believe that teaching involves only content material. This is an impression that they have received from their days at school. To be sure, teaching in the church school involves content material such as the catechism, the ritual of the church, and the

Bible; but to limit teaching to this is to fail at the task facing the church. To be successful the church, through its workers, must understand motives, attitudes, roles, and even the meaning of religious fellowship.

Needs, drives, attitudes, opinions, values, character, personality—these are words of common usage in our everyday world. Sometimes they seem to have meaning, but sometimes they seem to be used in such diverse ways as to defy definition. What is their meaning? Do they stand alone, or is there a relationship between the idea expressed by one of these words and the ideas expressed by others?

"Meet the needs of your children" is a statement often read or heard by both parents and church workers. That children have a need for love, or for security, or for recognition can be heard in many conversations. Everyone has a need for food. Does the word "need" have the same meaning when it is used for food as when it is used for security?

Sex drive, drive for achievement, drive for recognition are common usages of the word "drive." This word seems to have the meaning of a force with which we are born and about which we can do nothing. What is the meaning of this word; is it true that a drive is a natural force against which we are helpless?

We make judgments of the attitudes and opinions of our friends, neighbors, leaders, and teachers. We argue with others in an attempt to change their opinions and attitudes. Ministers preach from the pulpit in an attempt to persuade members of congregations to change their opinions and attitudes. We try to teach our children to have proper attitudes about other people, the church, the Bible, our nation, and a host of other things. Whence comes an attitude? Can we teach proper attitudes, and can we persuade others to change theirs?

There is much written and spoken today about the changed values of this nation. Much of the teaching we do in our homes and in our churches attempts to instill in our children and in our young people values which we hold dear and believe to be changeless. How are they learned? Perhaps if we understand the nature of values, we will be better able to teach them.

Character! This word seems to express something fundamental. The character of a man is his integrity. It is his good name. It is his belief in, and demonstration through deed of faith, basic moral values. We talk about teachers molding character. What are we talking about? Can character be molded or changed, or is it inherited from parents?

"What a personality!" "He doesn't have an ounce of personality." "If you aren't careful, you will warp your child's personality." These are representative usages of the word "personality," which is used so often and in so many different ways that it may have no meaning. The psychologist uses this word differently from its ordinary usage. He uses it to express an interplay of all the ideas expressed by need, attitude, value, and character.

For many years men have discussed the questions and

ideas presented above. Answers to the questions have come from those who have observed the actions of others and have attempted to find some meaning to it. Some of these persons were accurate and keen observers. Others were poor observers. Over a period of years, even centuries, we have arrived at commonsense notions about man's attitudes, values, character, and personality. Like many commonsense ideas, those about man are a mixture of true and false. It was not until we began to make accurate records of our observations and to apply the modern methods of science to these records that our knowledge of the behavior of man began to increase. Though we are still only on the threshold of knowledge about man and his behavior, what we do know can be of immense use to us. In the chapters which follow, information from the field of social psychology will be presented which will provide insight into many of the questions posed above and also many other questions concerning man as a social being.

What is social psychology? It stands at the boundary between a psychology which studies only the individual being and the sciences of anthropology and sociology which study man only as a member of a culture. Social psychology is concerned with the impact of culture on the individual and the individual's impact upon culture. It is both individual and group centered.

Individuals in a group or culture perpetuate those things they believe in and their way of life by teaching the babies and children the beliefs, customs, and ways of life they live. In order to understand an individual we must understand not only what he learned from his culture but how he learned from his culture. In this book we will look at attitudes, values, personality, self-hood, and the like, and also the formation of these through the impact of older members and peer members of the group upon the individual.

ONE

EXPLAINING HUMAN ACTIONS

Explaining the actions of others is one of the favorite games in which we indulge. When someone does something which we believe is out of character, we ask, "Why did he do it?" The newspapers, magazines, and books have many articles attempting to explain the reason for human actions. Before attempting an explanation of behavior, let us look at some of the inadequate explanations of the actions.

INSTINCT AND HUMAN ACTIONS

Instinct is often used to explain human actions. This word actually has many meanings. We hear someone explain, "I instinctively put my foot on the brake pedal." Obviously this refers to a highly developed, learned habit. Another use is illustrated by the phrase, "He has an instinct to achieve." Is there such an instinct as this, or is this an example of something that is learned? The drive for achievement is probably learned. In fact, the evidence is that man has no instincts at all.

Before the discussion is carried further, a definition of instinct is in order. *An instinct is an unlearned, relatively constant, chain of reflexes.* When the proper chemical change in an animal's body occurs, it sets off a chain of unlearned reflexes. The animal has no choice. The instincts are automatic and constant from one animal to another of a species.

One of the reasons for survival of human beings on this earth is their ability to change with changing conditions. Their behavior is flexible, much more so than that of animals. There is probably no animal which can survive a rapid change from life in the tropics to life in the arctic. A man can take off from an airport in warm New Zealand and in a few hours disembark at an airport in Antarctica and survive. Man can live in the atmosphere at sea level and yet survive—with proper equipment—one hundred miles above sea level. He can do this because of a lack of instincts rather than because of instincts. Man is flexible because of his great capacity to learn. Lower animals have instincts which are so inflexible that they cannot survive rapid changes in their environment. Instinct cannot be used to explain human behavior.

HEREDITY AND HUMAN ACTIONS

"Like father, like son." "A chip off the old block." "Blood is thicker than water." These are folk sayings which refer to the influence of heredity on human actions. Some people attribute most human traits to heredity. Others say that man is the result of what he has learned. What actions of men are influenced by heredity, and what actions are influenced largely by environment?

What is passed on from generation to generation? We inherit from our parents and from our parent's parents certain basic capacities such as intellect, muscle coordination, eyes sensitive or insensitive to color, ears more or less sensitive to sound, and certain temperamental traits such as tranquility. What is inherited is important, but to teacher and parent it is more important to consider how these basic capacities are developed and used by the individual. Children act like their parents, not because of what they inherited, but because of what they learn from their parents. Whether a high intelligence is used for the advancement of the kingdom of God or to its detriment depends upon lessons learned from parents, neighbors, teachers, and church school workers.

Which is more important—heredity or environment? This question cannot be answered because both are necessary. Without heredity we could not be born. Without environment we could not survive. In this book we shall be concerned with learning from our environment, but this emphasis is not intended to deny the effect of heredity. The concern is always with the interaction between them.

19

HUMAN NATURE AS AN EXPLANATION
OF BEHAVIOR

Have not we all heard the expression, "It's human nature for people to act that way," or "Human nature can't be changed"? Usually these statements imply that there is a basic or underlying pattern imposed on man by nature that forces him to act the way he does, a pattern of behavior from which man cannot escape. Certainly there are some things that man must do. He must eat, sleep, sneeze, breathe, drink water, and eliminate. It is possible also that man must react to frustrations with aggression, that man must relate himself to others, and that man must have sexual expression. These acts are in the nature of man, but they are also in the nature of dogs, monkeys, and other animals.

To confine the definition of "human nature" only to the above acts is to ignore the intricate group interrelations, the arts, music, science—things which distinguish man from lower animals and man in one culture from man in another culture.

The way that the members of one species of lower animals fulfill their biological needs is much the same from one locale to another. This is not true of man. All men need water, but there is a large difference between what water you will accept to drink and what the Australian aborigine will drink. All men need food, but there is a difference between the food on a dinner table set with crystalware and silver and the northern Indian stripping and eating the raw flesh from the still warm body of a deer.

The phrase "human nature" has too many meanings to be used in describing human behavior. Some of the meanings of "human nature" overlap with the meanings for heredity and learning. Other meanings of "human nature" are incorrect because they infer likenesses between human beings which are not univesral. We may reject "human nature" both as an explanatory and as a descriptive term having value for the understanding of human behavior.

IF NOT HUMAN NATURE, HEREDITY, OR INSTINCT—THEN WHAT?

At the present state of knowledge it seems evident that instinct has little influence over the actions of humans. The clue to understanding of human actions lies in the flexibility of human behavior, a flexibility which is the result of our being able to learn from our environment. The rejection of the place of instinct in determining human actions and traits of personality disturbs some people. They seem to feel that heredity and instinct are ways God has of guiding his people. Scientists should not tamper with them. These people fail to see that man with inflexible instincts and hereditary traits loses the one quality which distingiushes him from animals; that is, responsibility for his choices. The animal responding to an instinct has no choice; he must act. The lack of instinct in man, the necessity for learning to make the correct decision, has placed upon the teacher of man the responsibility for his actions.

TWO

THE LEARNING OF MOTIVES

In the previous chapter it has been inferred that man
is what he is because of his ability to learn from his environment. More important yet is the process of communicating the knowledge learned by one man to another. Learning is the key to the flexibility of mankind.
It is also the area in which the church worker is most
concerned. Since learning is so important, let us take
a brief moment to look at how we learn.

PHYSIOLOGICAL NEEDS

The food which we eat is burned by the body. The
water which we drink is used up. There is a world
around us that we must explore visually. There is some-

thing inside the body that changes and leads to the activity of the person. This change may be in the tissues of the body as they affect the nervous system, or it may be in the nervous system as it affects the organs of sight, hearing, touch, and taste. The changes that occur in the body tissue are called *needs* or *drives*. The needs or drives do not themselves lead us to food or water. They merely stimulate us to action. This is best illustrated by watching a very young infant. When the infant needs food, water, changing, cuddling, or a pin removed, he becomes restless and agitated. He does not know what he wants. Drive or need leads to activity or restlessness. In the infant this activity is undirected.

There are several of these primary needs or drives. Physiologists and psychologists have not decided upon their exact number. The needs or drives that are widely recognized today are hunger; thirst; elimination; exhaling of carbon dioxide; visual, auditory, and tactual exploration of the world. The sex drive is also often included in the primary drives. The needs or drives merely lead to activity. They do not determine the specific activity engaged in. We learn the ways in which these drives may be satisfied. We connect a drive or need with a specific activity which serves to reduce and diminish the need. The reduction of the need by this activity in some way serves to ingrain this activity in our nervous system so that when we have the same need again, we will engage in the activity which leads to the diminishing of the need.

The process of learning may be diagramed in this way.

Need or drive→→→cue from the environment→→→response

Hunger→→→mother's footsteps→→→feeding

An infant becomes hungry—need. He hears mother's footsteps coming—cue. A bottle (food) is given which reduces or diminishes the need or the drive. After this has occurred many times the infant will respond to the cue from the environment (mother's footsteps) as a signal that satisfaction of the need (food) is on the way. If he is crying, he will cease when he hears the footsteps. The infant has learned his first lesson. Of course, learning through life is more complicated than this, but this will serve our purposes for the present.

WHAT ARE MOTIVES?

The illustration of the infant learning the connection between hunger need and a bottle also illustrates the learning of a motive. A motive is a need plus the object or situation which diminishes the need.

Need + situation or object = motive

Motives in the infant are relatively simple. In the adult they are very complex. However, motives in both infants and adults represent the same learning process; the learning of the bond between a need and goal which will satisfy the need.

24

Is this what we mean when we say, "What is his motive for doing that"? It is true that the baby learning the connection between feelings of hunger and a bottle of milk seems to have little relation to the motives of adults; but if we examine the adult motive, it is the same. When we say, "What is his motive for doing that?" we are asking what inner drive has he that "makes" him act the way he does. A blunt way of saying it is, "What's in it for him?" What is in it is a satisfaction of a complex need. The action is a way of satisfying this need. The difference between the infant's motives and the adult's motives is the complexity of the need and situations and emotions accompanying satisfaction of the need.

There are other differences between adults and infants in motives. In the infant the need leads toward a goal which is a satisfaction of a physical requirement of the body. The goal is a physical object. In adults the needs themselves are learned from society, and the goals which are learned are seldom physical objects. Adult goals are almost always related to a change in the interactions between people.

Another great difference between infants and adults is in the time lapse between the need and the satisfaction of the need. In infants the time between the onset of the need and the satisfaction must be short, as any parent who has tried to warm a bottle in the wee hours of the morning will testify. The time lapse between the need and the attainment of the goal in adults may be many years. The young man who heeds the call to the ministry may spend four years in college and three in seminary before he attains his goal.

There is an important aspect of the learning of motives which must be considered at this point. Accompanying needs, their satisfaction, or their frustration is feeling or emotional tone. When we are hungry and then fed sufficiently, we feel good. There is a pleasant emotional tone which pervades the "need + situation or object." The emotional tone is learned as part of the whole situation. The completed diagram follows:

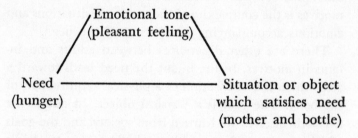

Emotional tone (pleasant feeling)

Need (hunger) ———————— Situation or object which satisfies need (mother and bottle)

People are motivated. They do not act from chance. They are going somewhere to do something. They have needs that they are trying to satisfy. In short, all the behavior of people is goal-directed. In order to understand them we must understand the nature of the needs for which satisfaction is sought, the goals which satisfy these needs, and the emotional tone which colors the whole process.

THREE

THE FORMATION OF ATTITUDES

Learning of motives is the first step toward the learning of attitudes. Attitudes are formed because many motives may be centered around one object. This may be illustrated by an individual worker in the church. The needs of the church become the needs of the diligent churchman. The nursery department has to have new tables. The churchman helps build them. A special offering for missions is needed. Our churchman makes this his need and satisfies this need by giving. A boys' class is without a teacher. The churchman is motivated to teach this class. The church, as an object, is the central focus of all these motives of this individual, the churchman. When many motives are centered in one object, an attitude is inferred. The attitude is not the action toward the object, but it is the preparation to act. The churchman in the illustration above has an attitude

27

toward the church as evidenced by his action. From watching the actions of the churchman over a period of time, an organizing or preparation for actions toward the church is evident. This organizing or preparation for action is a positive attitude toward the church.

When learning was discussed, the terms "need," "response," and "noticing the environment" were used. The term "response" requires further elaboration in order to understand the full range of meaning of the word "attitude." Responding may be in many forms: thinking, feeling, and perceiving. In other words a response is more than a series of muscle movements. If the example of the churchman in the preceding paragraph is examined further, it can be seen that while he acted by using muscles, his actions were guided by what he thought. He acted and thought the way he did because of his basic positive feeling toward the church.

More attention should be devoted to the word "feeling." Emotion is a very necessary part of attitudes. Too often an attempt is made to minimize the emotions of everyday living. Emotions or feelings are very much a part of us. They are in action in all that we do. It is an error to say that thinking or actions are without emotions. As the learning of motives occurs, the learning of the feeling tone that surrounds the need and the goal takes place. Since the goal is so often approval of others, the feeling of being accepted or rejected is learned as a part of the learning of the goal or the satisfaction of the need.

The word "perceiving" requires explanation. Perceiving, as it is used in psychology, means more than seeing. Perceiving means the receiving of sense impressions from the ears, eyes, nose, fingers, and the remainder of the senses and the making of meaning of those impressions. Perceiving is thus a dual process, receiving the sensation and making meaning of it. This is what is meant in Isa. 42:18, "Hear, you deaf; and look, you blind, that you may see!" Or what is meant in Matt. 13:16, "But blessed are your eyes, for they see, and your ears, for they hear."

By using the ideas presented in the previous paragraphs, the definition of attitudes may be summed as follows: *An attitude is a preparation to think, feel, perceive, and act in a certain way toward an object, person, institution, or idea.*

Of vital interest to church workers is a knowledge of the way that attitudes are formed. When learning is spoken of, the thought usually arises that a formal, deliberate attempt has been made to teach someone something. Most of human learning is not the result of a deliberate or logical effort on the part of parents, teachers, or other members of society. We learn a little bit at a time. Minute by minute situations are the building blocks of learning. Learning occurs when it is least suspected. Attitude formation is a process of learning. Some attitudes are taught by a more or less deliberate process, but most attitudes are learned from the thousand and one interpersonal relationships that occur each day in life.

Attitudes are learned when the person perceives that something in the environment has value for him. The value of the object is determined by the number of times it serves to satisfy needs, or in many cases the number of times the object is perceived in the face of punishment. The attitude toward mother may be used as an example of this. When the infant's need for cuddling is satisfied, mother is there. When the infant is thirsty, mother brings the water. Mother is not the substance that alleviates these needs, but she is present each time the need is satisfied. There is a pleasant feeling each time she is there. She becomes very valuable because she helps satisfy the needs of the infant.

In ways such as this attitudes toward material objects, persons, groups of persons, and institutions of society are formed. The value of the object, person, group, or institution to the learner is pointed out by direct satisfaction of needs, by words that carry emotional tone, and punishments that are given by parents or other members of the society. Perhaps dominant in all of this is the emotional tone present during this learning. When we listen to someone, we pay attention both to the words and to the emotional tone of the voice. Both are equally important to understanding. Illustrations of the formation of attitudes toward aspects of our religious life may illuminate this process.

Attitudes are formed toward valued objects. The value of an object is determined by its use to the individual and the number of times the individual sees it as valuable. In our religious life the Bible is a valued object. How is the attitude toward it formed, and what sort of attitude may be formed under different conditions?

A child sees the Bible only at Sunday school and church. Teachers and the pastor use emotionally toned words to illustrate the value of this book and the manner in which it is to be handled. The Bible is not to be found in the home of the child. What sort of attitude is likely to result from these circumstances? The child learns the Bible is a mystical book valued only in the church building.

In another home the child is well acquainted with the Bible. It sits on a stand in the living room. True, mother and father seldom open it, but they refer to it with words which indicate the Bible has a great value. This child sees the Bible used in Sunday school and in church and hears people speak in words which indicate the Bible is very important. What attitude has the child learned toward the Bible? The attitude would probably be centered around the Bible as a book and not around the Bible as a usable book or the content of the Bible. Undoubtedly, the child would note that many other books and objects, like newspapers and magazines, are used more often than the Bible. Father and mother read parts of the newspaper each day. They are cross when one of the children misplaces their magazines. The child may easily compare the emphasis placed upon the Bible with that placed upon other books or newspapers. He develops the attitude that the Bible has mysterious qualities. It does something in the home just to have it there.

It is not to be used for daily living as you would use the newspaper or magazine.

In another home the Bible is a well-used object. The children see it used and hear its words during family devotions. The children see their parents reading from it during other periods in the day. Bible study is a lesson, requiring work each evening just like school lessons. The attitude toward the Bible under these conditions would be different than the attitudes in the paragraphs above. In this family the Bible is valued because it is used. The value springs from the content of the book and not the mysterious quality of the book as an object.

Attitudes toward persons are also learned. Children learn to act differently toward different people. If the child has had warm, pleasant relations with his parents in his early months and years, it is likely that he will carry this attitude into new situations. He will see other persons as likely to be warm and friendly. On the other hand, if the child is reared in an atmosphere where he feels rejected, he is likely to meet others with the feeling that they will reject him. More about this particular subject will be covered in a later chapter.

Attitudes toward other groups are learned. These attitudes are learned in the same subtle ways illustrated above. A child goes down the street to play. When he comes home, mother says, "I don't want you to play with those children again. They aren't our kind of people." It is not so much what mother said as the way that she said it. The child has learned to pay attention to the emotional quality of the words. Mother points out the value of other groups by the way in which she speaks of them. However, the attitude is not learned in one occasion. Mother, father, teacher, or playmates— all contribute occasions to the learning of such attitudes. Each occasion may be only seconds long, but the impact of hundreds of these occasions results in the formation of a lasting attitude toward a group of people.

Attitudes are formed toward institutions such as church, school, college, marriage, family, and the like by the thousands of occasions an individual comes in contact with the institution, hears about it, or reads about it. A child learns about church not only from his parents but from the remainder of society. From his parents a child may learn that a church is an object, not an institution. It is a building to which you go once a week in order to be made to feel better. Society in general may reinforce some of the attitudes toward church. Along the highway are found signs, "Go to the church of your faith." Pictured on the sign is an object which is recognized as a church. An individual may learn the value of the church from the number of times it is called to his attention. How it is called to his attention is also pertinent. Many times the church is pictured as an object. Attending church is going to an object. It is not sharing worship with others, or sharing a rich cultural heritage. The attitude learned is toward the object, the church, not the institution.

ATTITUDES ARE NECESSARY
FOR COMMUNICATIONS

Attitudes are a very basic part of communications between persons. We ordinarily think of communicating only about objects or situations. However, the attitudes centering around these objects make communication possible. Did you ever try to talk about the Bible with someone whose attitude was that the Bible was an instrument to enslave people? Think of talking about the church with someone whose attitude is antagonistic toward the church. You are talking about the same object, but the contrary attitudes make communication impossible. One of the purposes of teaching religious beliefs in the home and in the church school is to build a common set of attitudes so that members of the religious community may communicate with each other about their religious experiences. How do children learn this common set of attitudes?

Parents talk to each other and to the children about situations arising in everyday living. When the child wants to talk to the parents about this same situation, he must use the same words as the parents to be understood. For example, mother says, "When you want a cookie, ask for it." Later the child says, "Mother, give me a gazebo." Since he did not use the same word as mother, she cannot know to give him a cookie. If, on the other hand, the child uses the word mother used, "cookie," he is more likely to be rewarded by receiving a cookie.

As we noted previously, the meaning of spoken words is carried both by the words and their emotional tone.

A child must learn to communicate both by words and emotional tone. For example, when we speak of God, our voices have certain emotional overtones. When children use the same emotional overtones, they are rewarded. If they use other emotionl overtones in speaking of God, they may be reprimanded. Reward is received when the attitudinal components of the communication are proper. Punishment or nonreward is received when the communication is not proper.

SYSTEMS OF ATTITUDES

In the previous section attitudes were treated as if they were independent of each other. Rather than existing independently, attitudes are tied together in systems. 1374484

The term "religious attitude" is often heard. This implies that only one religious attitude exists; whereas in recent research work many religious attitudes are found. They are found in systems of attitudes which include not only attitudes directly concerned with the church, God, and the Bible but also attitudes toward science and other things normally thought of as outside the realm of religion. Thus we may find an attitude toward science related to attitudes concerning the existence of God, the nature of the laws of science, and relations with other people—all within one system of attitudes. In research which was carried out by the author at least ten systems of attitudes were found which in some way related religious attitudes to one another, to attitudes toward morality, to attitudes toward science, and to attitudes toward one's self.

Two important questions may be asked at this point. Should the sincere Christian have several systems of attitudes? Should the sincere Christian unify many systems of attitudes into one system which ties the meaning of all life into the knowledge and love of Christ?

FOUR

THE FORMATION OF ROLES

In a sense every meeting with another person is a new event, even when we know the person. We have never met this person on this particular day in exactly these circumstances. In another sense the meeting is not new. Humans have the ability to categorize the events of their lives into systems of similar events. We sort the events of life into old, familiar categories. It is as if we were sorting a basket of mixed fruit into the several kinds of fruit. Apples are placed into one pile. Oranges are placed in another. This is part of the process of perception which was explained in an earlier chapter. Making meaning of events is placing them into familiar categories.

People who act alike are placed in the same category. Individuals who are dressed in white, feminine, found in hospitals, and have certain prescribed duties are placed in the role which is labeled nurse. The actions of the nurse are prescribed by society. Society tells the person in the role of nurse what she may do, what she is obligated to do, and what she may not do in relation to classes of persons called patients and doctors. Society prescribes standards of performance and the values to which the nurse must conform. The actions of a woman when she is in the role of nurse are prescribed in some detail by society.

Society not only prescribes the duties and obligations of the nurse; it also prescribes the attitudes and values of the nurse and the remainder of society toward the nurse. The nurse must have certain attitudes toward doctors and patients. A value which is expected of nurses is the obligation of compassion toward those who need help. We as members of society give certain deference to, and expect certain actions of, nurses when they are in their role.

What must the minister do to fulfill his role in society? Many actions may be listed, such as preaching, visiting the sick, talking to persons about their relations to God, and even acting in a somewhat subdued manner. There are attitudes and values which the minister must have. He is expected to love people, abhor gambling and swearing, see the best in others, and believe in the sanctity of the church. The primary values which we expect of him are the worth of the individual and the belief that this worth is endowed by God.

When a person assumes a role, society prescribes the

obligations the person owes to other members of society and the obligations society owes to the role-taker. This is true whether the role is informal, such as mother or father, or is formally prescribed by law, such as the role of doctor or lawyer.

ROLES ARE NECESSARY FOR COMMUNICATION

Roles not only tell us what to do when we are playing a particular role, they also provide us with a means of communication about persons. When the word "minister" is used, both the speaker and the hearer know what actions describe the minister. In order to communicate about the role of the minister one must know not only the label but also the actions which go with the label.

The child learns about roles by communicating about them. He sees a man bring a letter to the door and comments on the appearance of the milkman. Mother corrects him by saying this is the mailman and pointing out the difference in the actions of the two roles. Thus the child learns the many actions which fit under one label. Later the child may use the role-label to stand for all the actions of the role.

ROLE DEFINITIONS AND INTERLOCKING OF ROLES

A role has no definition by itself, but is defined always in terms of other roles with which it interlocks. Father is defined in terms of mother and children. Minister is defined in terms of parishioners. Teacher is defined by children, principals, and superintendents. When a person is taking a role, he is defined by the prescribed actions for that role and the way that role interlocks with others. Since much of life is spent in taking one role or another, the effects of role-taking upon the personality of an individual are important to consider.

ROLES AND SELF-CONFIDENCE

Society not only prescribes the actions of persons in a role, but also it prescribes the deference that society gives to persons taking a certain role. When we say a role has high prestige, we mean that society gives high value to those who hold this role. When it is said that a role has low prestige, it means that members of society give low or even negative value to it. All of us are acquainted with the value that society gives to a role. When a man is in a role to which society gives negative value—for example, garbage collector—he knows of the negative value. Because society gives negative value to the role, the man may give himself negative value. In essence the man may say to himself, "Since others don't think much of garbage collectors, and I am a garbage collector, I'm not worth very much." His personality is affected by the role which he takes.

RIGIDLY DEFINED ROLES

Some roles cause inner conflict and lack of confidence because they are too rigidly defined. They act as a straitjacket. They specify in great detail what the person must do and what he must not do. Such roles cause conflict because members of society know the exact boundaries of the role and are able to see any deviations from it. Deviation results in censure. Not only are members of society able to see deviations from the role, the role-taker himself is able to know when he deviates from the dictates of the role and may have feelings of guilt because of this.

An example of such a rigidly defined role is that of the minister in many communities. The community defines what the minister must do, including the style and color of his clothing. He cannot wear "loud" colors. He must never display anger. Personality conflict occurs in these circumstances because the minister can no longer be an individual.

THE EFFECT OF POORLY DEFINED ROLES

An individual's personality is influenced by the way that society defines his role. Some roles are marked by their stable, adequate definition. A person in a role knows what he is to do and what to expect from others. This knowledge should result in security and stability on the part of the individual. Unfortunately, many roles in our society are marked by both instability and lack of adequate definition.

The instability of roles and their lack of definition is a problem which touches each of us. Many of the problems of inner stress and conflict, of interpersonal conflict, and of the feeling of meaninglessness have their source in poorly defined roles; roles which are defined

41

poorly because of material and social changes in our culture.

Since one role defines another, as wife defines husband, if one changes the other must also change. If a primary role in society changes, such as the feminine role, the definitions of many interlocking roles change, and during this period of change all the interlocking roles are poorly defined.

How do these changes that create poorly defined roles affect us as individuals? They affect us because we can no longer predict adequately how others will accept us. The role is defined poorly when a given action which we believe is required by the role leads to acceptance and approval on one occasion and rejection or disapproval on another occasion. The ill-defined role has conflicting demands. At one time the role demands that we believe and act in a certain way and at other times it seems to require the opposite. In the individual this conflict causes stress and anxiety because he is unable to predict whether he is doing the correct thing or not. Between persons this conflict causes breakdowns in communication, since a person is never certain if the other person understands him.

Two of the dominant roles in American culture (the feminine and masculine roles) are marked with this inner conflict and breakdown of interpersonal communication. It is unnecessary to go into any great detail about the changing of the feminine role. Technological changes, the feminist movement, the flow of women into factories and business due to manpower shortage have all placed women in situations either taboo in the older feminine role definition or situations not covered by the older definition.

Since roles are defined as they interlock with other roles, those roles interlocking with the feminine role have changed definition as it has changed. The roles of wife and mother are changing, and this change has been marked by changes in the whole pattern of family life and child rearing. Since the masculine role is defined in part by the feminine role, changes in the latter cause changes in the former. The fact that conditions of life are changing has caused other changes in the masculine role. For example, our nation has changed from a pioneer and agricultural nation to an industrial and urban nation. The demands for physical strength and prowess which were necessary in a pioneer and agricultural life are not necessary today, and there has been a resulting de-emphasis on this part of the masculine role.

Another ill-defined role is that of the adolescent. Society demands both that the adolescent "act like an adult" and "remember that you are not yet an adult." The adolescent is urged to make his decisions and at the same time to remember that father and mother must be consulted and that they control the finances and the car.

What has this to do with the individual? These changes are marked by personality disturbances in the individuals that make up society. The changing role results in individual difficulties because the training the individual receives for a role may fit him for the role of fifty years ago but not for today. The individual has difficulty because he does not know how to act when taking the role. Shall the young woman take the role of passivity in courtship or shall she be modern and show initiative? Is the young woman to prepare herself to work in business or industry or for work in a home? What happens when the young man who believes the woman's place is in the home marries a young lady who believes she can have a career and also be both wife and mother?

Such changing and ill-defined roles make for difficulties because the individual does not know what pattern of action to follow. On one occasion the individual will be rewarded by members of society for certain action. On other occasions the same actions will result in censure. Insecurity is the result when one cannot predict whether action will bring reward or punishment.

It may seem that we are totally bound by the roles we learn from society. However, some persons are able to transcend their roles. It is one of the glories of the Christian faith that those who believe in Christ find a new dimension in living. They transcend their present roles and make them limitless.

FIVE

WHO AM I?

It seems to each of us that we have always been. Few can remember the first realization that he is unique. For most this realization is buried deep in the experiences of childhood. It is the development of this sense of uniqueness, this sense of individuality, this "I" as I know myself that is the subject of this chapter. The sense of selfhood is learned by means of social interaction. Just as roles cannot be defined except in relation to one another, so must individuals define themselves in relation to one another.

What is the origin of the self, or what I call me? The self or me is so much a part of an adult it is difficult to realize that once he did not have a self. The sense of selfhood is learned by means of social interaction. The infant probably does not distinguish the limits of his body from material objects or mother or other persons. He develops a sense of the limits of the physical being or self by the differing responses he receives from acting upon the world. An infant lies in his crib and looks at his fist. He holds it there until he can no longer hold it. It drops to the crib. Soon the infant has rested and has raised the fist for further examination. What is happening is that the infant is receiving dual sensations, from the eye and from the muscles that are supporting the arm. The infant grasps a rattle. This gives a different feeling than when he grasps his hand or toe. There is a reciprocal feeling when he grasps himself that is not present when he grasps an inanimate object. Some things are always present. The fist is there. The feelings of tension of the muscles, of breathing, and of vision are there. Other objects are present only part of the time. Mother comes and goes. Even the crib is gone for periods of time. The infant learns to distinguish these physical sensations that are there all the time from other things present only part of the time. This constitutes a sense of physical selfhood. To pass from the stage of infancy to childhood and to adulthood the individual must add to this sense of physical selfhood a sense of selfhood gained from social interaction.

DEVELOPMENT OF SOCIAL SELF

When the adults in the social environment attend to the needs of the infant and child immediately upon their arousal, the adults are seen as extensions of the child's need and satisfaction system. This treatment of the child is not continued long because mother and father have other duties to perform. The adults begin to place barriers in the way of the satisfaction of the child's needs. One of the first of these is the attempt to gradually teach the child to eat and sleep on the same schedule as the adults. Other barriers arise because society insists that the child be taught such things as table manners, proper respect for adults, and the like. Thus the child begins to learn that the world around him does not exist solely as a satisfier of his needs. Since this world operates independently of the needs of the child, he is able to begin to mark off where his body needs end because they are under his control whereas much of the remainder of the environment is not.

Communications also serve the child in his separation of himself from the world. The child is called by a name which is distinct from that of anyone in his family. As he grows older and wishes to communicate about himself, he uses the same name that his parents have used. This is evidence that the child is beginning to objectify himself. He is able to refer to himself as if he were an object. Communication also aids because the child learns that other parts of the environment have names. They are objects, and since they have a name different from himself, they are not the same as he is. The parents themselves are part of this objective world. Just as each material object has certain characteristics which make it different from all other objects, mother and father have certain actions which are different from each other. The name "mother" goes with a certain set of actions and the name "father" with another set of actions. The child is learning to apply names to sets of actions which we have earlier defined as roles. Just as the child sets himself apart from other objects because they are different and have names different from his, so he sets himself apart from his mother and father.

In trying to satisfy his needs the child soon learns that there are certain conditions under which his needs can be satisfied. Little Albert says, "Mummy, I want a cookie." Mother replies, "No, not until after lunch." Mother attaches conditions to the obtaining of the cookie. Albert wishes father to play with him, but father says he will not play until he finishes the sports section of the newspaper. Albert is learning that under certain conditions his needs will be satisfied. As he grows older he is able to remember for longer periods of time. He can remember that he must not ask father to play with him when he has the paper in his hand. Mother rushes about all day cleaning the house. When Albert asks for mother's aid, she may say, "Not today, mother is busy. We will play tomorrow." The next time, or the next, this situation arises, Albert is able to predict that mother will not play with him today. Albert is learning to predict the actions of mother and father, and this is a step in building his sense of selfhood. It indicates to the child that mother and father are not completely under his control as his arms or legs are. Since they are not under his control, they are not part of him. He sets apart that which he can control as "me" and the parts that cannot be controlled as "not me."

The child learns and plays out roles such as milkman, soldier, father, and mother. The child has learned the distinctive behaviors which mark each of these roles. In a sense he is able to say, "I play milkman, but I am not a milkman. I am different." The child is defining himself through learning of roles. More importantly, he is learning to act like others; to do so he must "put himself in other's shoes." This is the beginning step toward consideration for others.

Learning consideration of others is a vital part of the definition of selfhood. It is the beginning of the child's realization that the world does not exist solely to satisfy him or that the world does not revolve around him. This step in the definition of selfhood may continue until the child is able to offer sympathy for others. As the child learns to predict the actions of mother and father, he begins also to be able to act out these actions for himself. The acting out of the role of another is a step in being able to put himself in another's place. It is a step in the direction of being able to say, "If I were in his position, I would feel badly." This is the beginning of sympathy.

Another step in the learning of selfhood is the learning of "dos and don'ts." "Don't run into the street." "Wash your hands." "Eat with your fork." "Don't talk back to your mother." At least some of these "dos and don'ts" are necessary to protect the child and to make him a member of society. A part of learning of selfhood is the learning of rules and regulations. The child makes a part of his self the rules and regulations of his group. He internalizes these "dos and don'ts."

A certain amount of frustration is a necessary part of these lessons. The child is frustrated when he must postpone need satisfaction. Frustration may result from learning consideration of others because his need satisfaction must be postponed.

Some parents feel that if you really "love" your child, you will not let him suffer frustration. These parents allow their children to fulfill needs whenever and wherever they arise. The child is not taught rules and regulations of society and to be considerate of others because to do so would frustrate the child. If parents always give in to the child, they are teaching him that the world exists solely to satisfy his needs.

Some have defined sin as self-centeredness because self-centeredness sets a world apart from God. The parent who never teaches the child consideration for others is helping to insure that this individual will have difficulty in knowing God because he cannot let go of the idea that he is the center of the world.

THE NECESSITY FOR CONSISTENCY

We have little difficulty in learning about the physical aspects of our environment because they are stable. Walls do not move when we walk into them. The earth upon which we walk is stable. Chairs remain the same from day to day. The perceptions of the physical world of the child are reinforced in the same way time after time because the physical object remains as it is.

The social world is not as stable as the physical world. Where are the brick walls of the social world? There are walls called rules, regulations, good manners, etiquette, moral standards, and laws. Unfortunately, these rules and regulations of social life are neither visible nor are they entirely stable and consistent. The child finds himself in a social world where he may on one occasion meet a social wall (his parents prohibit him from doing something), and on another very similar occasion find that no wall is there. How is he going to learn to predict whether there is a wall or not? Society attempts to teach youth its rules and regulations. In order to do so the parents that make up the society must teach these rules in a consistent way. Part of the rules of a society have to do with the actions called role actions or behavior. Society decrees there are certain ways that mothers shall act and certain ways that fathers act and certain ways that the child acts. The child can learn to predict the actions of mother and father only if they do the same things time after time. If they change their actions, the child has no way of building a set of predictions for their actions. We might predict that when the parents are not consistent in their actions, the child will have difficulty in literally defining "Who am I?"

GROUPS ARE NECESSARY FOR THE DEFINITION OF SELFHOOD

The family group is the first group in which the child begins to define his sense of selfhood. As the child goes beyond the home into neighborhood groups, he goes

51

through somewhat the same process of defining self in relation to other groups as he did with mother and father. As the child learns more roles through his interaction with age-mates, older children, and other adults, he is better able to define "Who am I?" The process might be likened to that of the stability of an object to sit on. If a stool has only two legs, it is somewhat unstable. Add another leg and it becomes more stable. Add several legs and it is even more stable. We might define the process further by listening to an imaginary conversation of the child as he plays in a group. He looks at one friend and thinks, "I am a little like Allen, but still, I am different. I am different from Susan. I am different from Jack though he does some things like me. I am different from all of these yet somewhat like them." Just as we see ourselves mirrored in others, so does the child. And just as we see ourselves as different from others, so does the child. It might be said that we cannot be different unless there are others to be different from. One cannot be a unique self without other selves to be different from. The family and other groups enable the child to develop an adequate sense of selfhood.

FEMININE AND MASCULINE ROLES

Certain roles are more important to children than others because their effects are widespread. The basic roles are the masculine and feminine. We interact with others first of all as masculine or feminine and secondly as a child, adolescent, adult, lawyer, doctor, or senator. Because the feminine and masculine roles interpenetrate all aspects of life, any difficulty in playing these roles has consequences in many areas of living. Difficulty in roles is the result of poor models in learning the role or of change in the role prescription within the culture. We have discussed in the chapter on roles the effect of the change in the culture.

Parents who do not have adequate knowledge of the masculine and feminine roles cannot teach them to children. Children learn masculine and feminine roles from both parents. A girl learns the feminine role from both her mother and father because the roles are mutually defining. From her mother she learns what it means to be a woman and how women react to men. From her father she learns how men interact with women. Boys learn the masculine role from both father and mother. From father he learns the activities and attitudes typical of men in our society. He learns to interact with men. From mother he learns how women interact with men. From her he learns what is traditionally feminine behavior, and this helps him define what is masculine by seeing the contrast between the two roles.

If you ask persons to answer the question "Who am I?" the first response that most of them give is almost invariably, "I am a boy," or "I am an American girl," or "I am a man." They use the sex role as a basic anchor to their self-picture. Inadequacy in defining oneself in the proper sex role creates difficulty in knowing "Who am I?"

As has been noted, roles, with their attitudes and values, are learned from parents, teachers, age-mates, and others. The system of attitudes which is most important to each individual and pervades all roles, attitudes, and values is attitude toward self. "How do I like myself?" "Am I likely to be successful, or am I doomed to failure?" Because these attitudes are concerned with self, and self is in every situation, what I think of myself cannot be escaped. The systems of attitudes toward self are learned early in life in the family. They are fairly permanent. This means that most persons carry attitudes toward self which they learned in childhood for the remainder of their lives.

The word "self" has been used throughout this chapter without defining the word explicitly. The self is I, John Smith, as I know John Smith to be. The accent is on the word *know*. The self is the physical part of me of which I am conscious. It is the image I have of my physical features. It is my feeling of security or insecurity in facing the situations of my world. Self is what I believe, my conscious attitudes, roles, and values. It is both what I know myself to be and what I hope myself to be.

SIX

THE LEARNING OF VALUES

Of great interest to church workers is the growth of
values. For many years psychologists, in their attempt
to be strictly scientific, did not consider the study of
values. In recent years, however, more and more attention has been given to this study. The task of the psychologist in the study of values is not to determine their
rightness or wrongness. This is the task of religion. The
psychologist's task is to determine under what conditions values are learned and what effect they have upon
the personality. This section will examine these points.

In previous chapters we saw how attitudes and roles
are learned. Stress was placed upon the learning of attitudes and roles from groups. It was pointed out that
learning of roles from groups is necessary for the definition of self. The self is seen within the framework of

groups. The self is defined in terms of a group, and since the self is part of the group, the group is somewhat defined in terms of the self.

We say, "This is my group." When we are in the group, we see ourselves as a member of the group. Our group is different because we see ourselves as members and because there are other groups of which we are not members. Our group is different from other groups, as we see it, because we are part of it. Because we include ourselves in the group, the group is defined partly in terms of our being members. The group is a part of us just as we are a part of it.

Needless to say, the self is valuable. The longer each of us lives with his individual self, the more valuable it becomes. Part of the value of self is dependent upon the group because the group gives definition to self. It provides us with roles, attitudes, values, and satisfies some of our needs. Therefore, the self perceives groups of which it is a member as being valuable.

The groups of which we are members have habitual or traditional ways of interacting, and they have goals which we accept. The traditional ways of interacting (rules and regulations) become for the individual members of a group not just a way of acting but the proper way to act. The group's rules and regulations become standards for individuals to uphold in their behavior. The goals of the group become a part of us and serve as goals toward which we strive. In the group the rules and regulations serve to keep the activities of the group oriented toward the goal. The goal thus gives meaning to and ties together the functions of the group. When the individual internalizes the group goal—that is, makes the group goal a part of selfhood—the goal serves the same function for him that it served for the group. It serves to give meaning for, and ties together the activities of, the individual.

The roles that are learned from the group may become part of our values. A group or society, in case of standard roles such as minister and lawyer, prescribes the actions which a person playing the role must perform, may perform, and must not perform. An individual may make the role action or behavior so much a part of himself that he sets up the prescribed actions as standards of behavior. If the individual talked to himself about this, he might say, "A good minister does these things and believes in this way. I will try to be a good minister by doing these things and believing in these ways." The individual sets the group's role prescription as a goal to be reached. This is a part of what is called values.

The Boy Scouts of America as an organization has rules, regulations, and prescribed behavior for its members. An individual, upon joining this organization, may say to himself, "To be a good Boy Scout I must help others." The individual is making an organizational goal his goal. He is setting an organizational goal as a standard or value to be attained. We wish our children to become a part of the church group for the same reason. We wish them to make the Christian goals of

57

the church their goals. Group rules, regulations, and goals thus may be internalized and become the values of the individual.

In watching individuals over a long period of time, we notice their attitudes are not specific to one situation. There is a continuity of action from one situation to the next. A church member has attitudes in church which are related to his attitudes outside the church. The church member is really not a different person outside the church from inside the church. There is a consistency in his attitudes and behavior. This consistency occurs in part because the individual sets for himself ideals. "I am a church member, and a church member should act in these ways." An individual's ideal way of acting is his value, a value which serves to integrate behavior in many different situations.

The rules, regulations, and roles of groups become the standards of ideal behavior for individuals. These values serve not only as a standard for acceptable actions on the part of the individual but also as standards to judge the actions of others. Values are used to judge both the individual's actions and the behavior of others. Just as the individual uses group goals as his goals, in the same manner he can and does judge others. "I am a good Sunday school teacher if I do certain things, but if I fail to do them I am not a good teacher." "She is not a good Sunday school teacher because she fails to prepare her lesson properly." The standards of a group are being used to judge another's behavior.

The rules, regulations, and roles of a group may be internalized by an individual to the extent that he no longer recognizes their source. Instead of saying, "To be a good church member I ought to help others," a person simply feels that it is right to help others and wrong not to help others. In fact, he feels he *ought* to help and that others *ought* to want to do the same.

At this point a definition of value can be given. *A value is a person's idea of what is desirable, what he or others ought to want, and what the self-behavior and behavior of others ought to be.*

THE FAMILY IS THE PRIMARY TEACHER OF CULTURAL AND RELIGIOUS VALUES

Most parents hope to teach their values to their children. Though parents may plan to deliberately teach values and books may imply that values may be taught deliberately, most children learn their values in the same subtle way they learn attitudes. They learn them from the day-to-day behavior of their parents and age-mates. They learn them from those situations which the parents emphasize by talking about frequently or showing strong emotion about. Parents talk about those things which interest or threaten them. Their emphasis on certain values comes from what basically interests or threatens the parents. A child may learn to overvalue material possessions because this seems to be the main topic of conversation between the parents. Social prestige may become a strong value for the child because the parents continually stress the necessity for pleasing those who have higher status and push the child into situations involving those of higher status. Success as a value is often taught by continually stressing the need for succeeding. The need for success may be stressed both by rewarding actions which the parents believe are successful and by punishing the child when he has not met the parent's ideal of success.

Values are sometimes defined in terms of achieving certain symbols. The acquiring of an education is such a value. Parents may emphasize the obtaining of the symbols of education, a diploma or a degree, as equivalent to education itself. The obtaining of money may become a value in itself because of the continual stress placed on having money.

Parents teach not only the values a child holds but also the culturally acceptable ways these values may be obtained. Most parents who teach the value of material possessions also teach the "proper" ways of obtaining these possessions. Very few parents teach that a person may obtain possessions by violent means. There are several paths to achieving the value of higher status and prestige. Obtaining more education is one route, and selecting a profession as a vocation is another such route. Many parents who comment when they send their child to college, "I want my children to have the things that I didn't," actually mean, "I want my children to have higher status and prestige which education can bring."

They do not mean, "I want my child to know the things I missed knowing."

Religious educators are vitally concerned about the teaching of values, and desire that children be taught to hold religious values as their primary values and to use religious values to unify their personalities. Since it is through the family that these values are taught to the young, the educators must work through the family to achieve this. Even though the principle of working through the family is adhered to by the religious educator, the task is a difficult one. The parent, in teaching values to the children, is acting out long-practiced habits of perceiving and acting toward others. These habits are difficult to eradicate, but to achieve success in teaching religious values some method must be employed to reduce the strength of these long-term habits of perceiving and acting. A parent or teacher must know his values in order to change them. "What do I believe?" "What do I value most?" These are questions which must be answered before the worker in the church or the parent can even plan the teaching of values. Since the changing of attitudes and values will be the subject of the final chapter, nothing more will be discussed about it here.

When we speak of values, we must not assume that they are what we *say* they are. Values are not words. Values guide words and actions. The real definition of a value is the action or behavior of a person. Values may be learned through words, but they are learned primarily through intensely personal relations with other persons. They are learned through identifying oneself with others and emulating their behaviors and decisions. A value is a thousand and one actions and an equal number of decisions. This is the reason that values are so difficult to teach.

VALUES AND MEANING

Much is read today of meaninglessness. Both older and younger people complain that life has no meaning. What gives life its meaning? In order for life to have meaning, we must know who we are. We must have developed an adequate sense of selfhood. Part of this sense of selfhood is value. To know who we are we must know what we value. What outside of me is valuable enough to commit my life to?

In previous chapters the effect of a changing society on roles and self was discussed. Changes in a society result in changing or at least reinterpreting the values of society. During a period of change an individual has difficulties in learning values because there are many different versions of the same value, or the value has been declared worthless by some contemporaries. It takes time for a society to develop its system of values. During a period of change the old values have been challenged and new values have not had time to become stable. Or old values have not had time to restabilize. In terms of the individual living in this society, it means that he has no real *oughts, ideals,* or *goals* with which to identify. Without these he cannot know himself. He cannot commit himself to that which is greater than himself because the older commitments are challenged or because possible newer commitments cannot be identified. Life is meaningless because the only meaning to life, our deepest values, are questioned.

SEVEN

PERSONALITY AND CHARACTER

Nearly every national magazine today contains some article purporting to reveal how to change personality, how to improve personality, how to keep from warping a child's personality, or the description of the personality of some famous person. These articles often give impressions of personality which are different from the findings of research psychologists and psychiatrists. When the psychologist talks of personality, he is using the word in a different sense than is used in ordinary language. For example, the psychologist does not talk about a person having *no* personality, or having a good personality. Every person has *a* personality, and the psychologist seeks to understand how it was formed and to describe what the personality is like. What the layman usually means when he says that someone has a good personality is that this person interacts well with others.

64

The psychologist must explain with the same laws both those who interact well with others and those who do not.

Psychologists use the following definition of personality. *Personality is the persistent organization of attitudes, values, routes to goals, ways of solving problems, and temperament factors.*

In our daily associations with people we must react to the uniqueness of personality. Our constant reactions to the differences between persons sometimes blind us to the knowledge that there are also a great many similarities. If careful notice were taken, more similarity than uniqueness might be found. What is the source of this similarity between persons?

The dress and the behavior of the members of one of the sexes shows great similarity. It might be supposed that the similarity in such a case is biological in origin. The study of the cultures of other peoples shows that what we consider masculine in action and dress in our society might be considered feminine in action and dress in another society. There are some behaviors which are similar throughout the human race, but these are basic biological needs such as coughing, sneezing, and elimination. The biological needs require no learning. The actions that make us distinctively human all require learning. Men within a certain culture are similar in action because they have learned to be similar. The traits that typify a group are passed on to the next generation by teaching. The traits which we believe are typically American are passed from generation to generation, father teaching son who in turn teaches his son. The similarities between the people of a society are learned similarities.

When the word "culture" is referred to, many persons think of something that exists apart from people. While it is true that many objects of culture exist, such as cars, dishes, chairs, guns, and the like, the real core of culture is the meanings that these objects and the actions of the people of a culture have for other members of the culture. What is studied by sociologists and anthropologists and called culture is the similarity in action between members of a community. The actions that are studied are part of what has been defined as personality. What we call our religious culture is seen in the actions or behavior, the personality, of those of our community.

PEOPLE ARE DIFFERENT

In the previous section the stress was placed upon the likenesses in personality. It is noticeable that people are not only similar throughout a society but also different. The similarities were accounted for above by action of the family in passing the culture from generation to generation. The uniqueness in personality must also be accounted for. One of the sources of uniqueness is biological, each person being different from any other person because of his heredity. To some extent each person has a set of intellectual, temperamental, and muscular capabilities different from any other. The manner in which these capabilities are developed depends upon the unique history of the individual. No individual has a history of life events quite like anyone else. We are born into a certain family in a certain city, nation, and culture. Our interactions with other people are unique in the sense that we have parents, brothers, sisters, and friends who are unique.

The family into which a child is born is unique. Each of the parents is unique genetically, and each has a unique series of experiences in dealing with the world of which he is a part. They have solved the problems which the environment has presented them in unique ways, and they teach their children what problems are likely to be faced in the world and how to solve these problems.

The parents have a unique set of values and goals, and since they are likely to see their children as an extension of themselves, they are likely to insist that the child attempt to fulfill this same set of values and goals.

Another aspect of life that makes for individuality is the different set of problems forced upon each individual by the parents and by culture. The parents, being individuals interacting with other individuals in a society, must meet the demands of these interactions at the same time they are rearing their children. The conflict that the parent feels is to some extent carried into the child-rearing situation and thus becomes a problem for the child to solve.

In every stable culture most of the problems faced by individuals in the culture have standard answers. Parents in the stable culture teach both the problem and the solution. The American culture is in the middle of change and presents to each generation many problems not faced by the previous generation. Many of the problems faced today were not dreamed of in past generations. Parents cannot teach the solution of specific problems and hope to make their children adequate for tomorrow because the problems of tomorrow may not be the same as the problems of the world of the parent. Parents must teach how to solve problems successfully. Part of the definition of personality given previously in this chapter included problem-solving methods.

What is a problem? For an individual a problem is a barrier in his way to a goal. The individual must go through, over, around, or remove the barrier in order to reach the goal. As children face barriers to goal progress, they learn habitual ways of dealing with barriers. These ways, or problem-solving methods, may continue throughout the lifetime of an individual. In other words, the individual attempts to solve new problems in the same manner as he solved former ones. An illustration of this might be a pattern of dependency. Ambrose's mother solved his problems for him. Even when Ambrose had difficulty with a toy, his mother would help him. As he grew older, he learned that anything that presented difficulty could be solved by calling loudly for mother. Mother became the standard solution to all his problems. Even in situations beyond the home, Ambrose soon learned there was someone to solve his problem for him. Either temper tantrums or rational problem-solving may be used by the individual just as dependency was used by Ambrose.

In a society in transition it is necessary for the good mental health of the individual that he learn rational problem-solving methods. It is even more vital for the religious groups in a society in transition for individuals to learn and use rational problem-solving methods in meeting the problems of the religious groups. Rational problem-solving methods will be learned and used by individuals if parents teach them and reward their use.

Different authors present a different number of steps in the problem-solving method. Four steps will be presented here. They are as follows:

1. Definition of the problem. It is reasonable that if one does not know what situation he is facing, he is not likely to solve his problem. Problems mean that a person is doing something to reach a goal and a barrier is in the way. In defining the problem the first step is to determine the goal. The second step is to find out what bars the way to the goal.

2. Preparation of several solutions to the problem. Knowing the goal and the nature of the barrier, a person should select several possible ways of arriving at the goal. More than one solution to the problem is prepared in case the first or the second alternative does not work. This is done in advance of actually testing the alternatives in the real situation for the very good reason that if the first solution does not work, one may become

frustrated and unable to think of any further alternatives.

3. Before the solutions are tested in the actual situation, they should be tested mentally to see if they are likely to work. In complex situations gathering of information may be necessary before the solutions may be tested mentally.

4. Those solutions which are found satisfactory in this test are tried in the actual situation.

This may seem like an elaborate process to attempt to teach children. However, it is not too unlike the process of problem-solving used by all of us. The crucial point is that a child should use it often enough for it to be available for his use when needed and that he be rewarded for using it. Children should not be rewarded for using dependency, aggression, threat, or other such means of reaching goals.

CONFLICT SITUATIONS INVOLVE INTERPERSONAL RELATIONSHIPS

Toys, sidewalks, and other inanimate objects that do not bend to the child's will may frustrate him. As he grows older, he learns that inanimate objects and physical events are not the major source of his frustrations. He finds that people are involved in his frustrations. Most of the time when an older child, adolescent, or an adult finds an obstacle in the way to a goal, this obstacle is in the form of another person or something said by a person. This has implication for personality.

An individual moving toward something he wants

(a goal) and suddenly being faced by a barrier may be diagramed as follows:

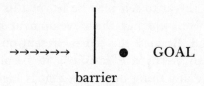

The manner in which the individual perceives—that is, sees and interprets—the barrier may determine whether he will solve the problem and reach the goal. The individual may see the problem objectively, even though the barrier represents another person, and use rational problem-solving methods. In using such he may do one of three things: (1) make a direct attack on the barrier, (2) go around the barrier, or (3) decide that further attempts to reach the goal are useless and accept a substitute goal. On the other hand, the individual may see the barrier as a personal threat to himself and begin to set up defenses against the barrier, thus abandoning the goal.

Many persons are set to perceive threat. Whenever they reach a barrier they immediately think, "Why is this man out to get me?" Their goal becomes defense or revenge against the man they perceive as the barrier. In using time and energy against this subgoal of revenge or defense, they have little or no time left for their original goal. The perceiving of a barrier as an objective problem to be solved or as a threat to the self may represent a persistent aspect of personality. As has been stressed, the habit of rational problem-solving is learned in the family. So, too, the perceiving of the barrier as a threat to self may be learned in the family.

In a previous chapter the development of selfhood was discussed. Because the self is present on all the occasions when needs are satisfied, it becomes highly valued. Like any thing or person that is highly valued, the self must be defended when it is under attack. When the individual perceives threat, he is perceiving a threat to self and sets up measures to defend the self. How is this self to be recognized? All of us have mental pictures of how we look physically, and also of how persons such as ourselves are to act on various occasions. This composite physical self-picture and self-ideal is what is called the self. We perceive that someone is threatening us when we feel they are trying to damage the self-picture we have. Some people as a result of childhood training are more prone to perceive threat to the self-picture than are others.

How do children acquire a readiness to perceive threat? They learn this in their early family experiences. Mothers and fathers would not deliberately set out to make a child perceive threat. However, many mothers and fathers in their minute-to-minute and day-to-day contacts with the child teach the child to perceive threat.

The child learns about his world through interpersonal relations. Even making meaning of the world of material objects is learned through interpersonal relations. The child asks, "What is this, mother?" and "What is that, mother?" many times a day. Mother's explanation teaches the child the meaning of the object world. The social world is learned in the same manner. Part of learning in the social world is what is called "growing up." What this means in action is that the child's previous ways of solving problems are no longer successful. When the child is first learning to feed himself, he is allowed to use his hands to help put the food in his mouth. As he grows older, the parents insist on his using a spoon; later, they teach him not to spill food on the table. Wetting and dirtying of pants is acceptable in the early stages of growth, but later it is prohibited. The child faces a continuous set of problems. This type of learning is necessary; and, as was pointed out in an earlier section, the differentiation of self from others is partly accomplished in this manner. Does this mean that the child is doomed to learn to perceive threat? Whether or not the child perceives a threat depends upon the way the parents teach these behaviors necessary for later childhood and adulthood.

PERCEIVING THREAT

Some parents attempt to teach impossible tasks too early in life. The child is forced to be neat and clean before he has control of the muscles necessary to accomplish the required actions. He is forced to use a spoon before he can hold one properly. He is forced into toilet training before he can control the muscles of elimination. He is forced to attempt to read before he has the necessary muscle coordination and vision with which to read. Since he has not developed enough to

73

do these, he fails more times than he succeeds. The parents force him into failure. Since the parents are people, the child may carry this feeling of certain failure into other situations involving people. Situations involving people thus become threats to the child because he sees himself as certain to fail. As was mentioned in a previous section in reference to problem-solving actions, problem-solving methods and attitudes learned in childhood may last throughout a lifetime. The readiness to perceive threat may persist throughout a lifetime.

Does this mean that the child should never experience failure? It certainly does not. Children need to experience failure because this is part of living. Those children who have not learned to accept failure in a positive way have as much difficulty in life as those who experience too much failure. But children should have a larger proportion of success experiences than failure experiences.

Parents may teach their children to perceive threat in other ways. Though it is necessary to learn the rules and regulations of life and these must often be taught by frustrating the child's previous responses, some parents make this process difficult for the child. They may recognize that children cannot perform certain actions until the muscles and nerves are developed enough to permit the action, and take account of this in their training. Yet they teach failure and threat to their children. They do this by making the child feel he is

74

rejected when he breaks one of the many rules and regulations which guide our lives. How often have we heard the comment from well-meaning parents, "If you do that again, mother won't love you any more"? Or the comment, "Naughty boys who do that are sent away"? What could be more threatening to a child than to be denied the love and presence of the parents? The parents form the only world the child knows, and to deny him this is to expel him from the only group in which the self has meaning. When it is necessary to frustrate or punish the child in order to teach necessary ways of doing things, the parent should attempt to make clear the punishment is for the act committed and not a rejection of the child as a person.

If there is not consistency in the teaching of the roles, rules, and regulations in a society the child may become insecure. Insecurity leads to the perception of threat from the world. Lack of consistency may result from many factors. Some parents, wishing to assure themselves of their children's love, allow their children freedom to do most anything they like. These parents, becoming exasperated at their children's actions or reacting to their neighbor's comments about too much freedom, will suddenly punish or prohibit their children from doing some things which they have been doing. These incidents occur time and time again until the child cannot predict whether he will be allowed to act or be punished for it. This is a state of insecurity.

Children who have received little knowledge of the rights of others will have difficulty in meeting the demands of the world outside the family. They attempt to use others outside the family for satisfying their needs in the same way they have used their parents. They meet with frustrations because other people do not wish to spend all their time satisfying the needs of one individual. Other people threaten them because they frustrate instead of satisfy their needs. These so-called spoiled children begin to perceive all other people as threats to their need satisfaction.

Some parents teach their children to be insecure because the parents themselves are insecure. The parents in their childhood learned insecurity. When they become adults their insecurity might show itself by their being overly loving for awhile to prove the child loves them and then rejecting the child when they feel the child does not love them. This sense of insecurity results in perceiving the world as threatening.

Parents may teach their children to perceive others as threatening in a direct manner. If the parent perceives other people as threatening, he will tell the child that this person is likely to hurt the child. If this is done often enough the child will begin to predict hurt from those categories of people whom the parent has pointed out. Some authorities have said that this threat of hurt from others is one of the main sources of prejudice.

IMPLICATIONS OF THREAT PERCEPTION FOR RELIGIOUS WORKERS

What are the implications of this for persons interested in the religious rearing of children? We believe and teach of the love of God and the brotherhood of man. One who is threat-oriented is perceiving others, not in terms of love, but in terms of fear and defense. A perception of and action toward other people as being worthy of God's love and our love is opposed to the perception of people as being a threat to the self. In order to love others we must first perceive them as recipients of our love, not recipients of our defense measures. Religious education must help families to rear their children so that they are able to love rather than to perceive others as threatening self.

But if we realize that we are threatened and made afraid by other people and external events, how can we cope with these fears and help reduce them? We are able to love without perception of threat to the extent that we perceive the assurance of God's love toward us. As Paul said, "I am sure that neither death, nor life . . . shall be able to separate us from the love of God" (Rom. 8:38-39). With the assurance that we cannot be separated from the source of all love, how can we be afraid?

These references to love and to perception of others through love does not mean that we are less rational in our thinking or that we are "looking at the world through rose-colored glasses." On the contrary the less our perceptions of others and our thinking are distorted by fear, the more we are able to eliminate threat perception from our lives. The acceptance of the assurance of God's love frees us to see the world as it is.

77

CHARACTER

Character is that part of personality that has to do with moral rules, regulations, and values. Let us take a brief look at the stages in the formation of character and the implications for church workers and parents. These stages offer convenient ways of summarizing growth in character. They are not to be regarded as having the power of forcing individuals to act a certain way in a certain stage. They are descriptive. Individuals progress through the stages because of interactions with others and what they learn from these interactions.[1]

Amoral. The infant learns motives through interaction with others. He regards others as extensions of himself. There is only one rule, that of need satisfaction. Though this is a stage in infancy, some adults seem to behave as if they were in the amoral stage. Their only concern is their need satisfaction, and others are seen only in terms of their help in achieving need satisfaction.

Expediency. The infant progresses out of the amoral stage by beginning to learn rules and regulations and to realize that others control need satisfaction. He learns to obey or to consider others to obtain need satisfaction. In a sense the expedient individual is saying, "I will consider your needs only because you now control need

---

[1] The titles of these stages are from *The Psychology of Character Development* by Robert F. Peck and Robert J. Havighurst (New York: John Wiley & Sons, 1960).

satisfaction." One may note that some adults seem to act in this manner.

Irrational-Conformity. As children begin to internalize the rules and regulations of adults, they move into a different stage. Parents and adults seem to have all the answers and power. They know the names of all objects. They describe what to do in all situations. They uphold the rules and regulations of society. In the face of such knowledge and power the child feels that he must conform in order to have satisfaction of needs. As he becomes a part of groups he begins to internalize the rules and regulations of the adult world.

If the demands of the parents for conformity are heavy and constant, the child will internalize the rules and regulations of the parents without examining the rational basis of such demands. Their conformity is irrational—without rational thought. This is the way the "puritan conscience" develops. Children obey rules and regulations because they have learned to conform. They are considerate of others because this is one of the rules they must obey. They have learned to obey the letter of the law.

Individuals may move away from this stage for several reasons. They may discover that not all needs can be satisfied by the laws learned from their parents. As the individual moves away from home influence into a larger community, he may find others who believe somewhat differently, and in order to communicate with them he must change. Parents may recognize that rigid con-

79

formity to rules and regulations is not good for the individual and for the community.

Rational-Altruistic. The final stage of character growth is rational-altruistic. Individuals move toward this stage when they become genuinely considerate of others. They can tolerate differences of attitudes and values in others because they, figuratively speaking, feel as if they were in the same situation. The individuals growing into this rational-altruistic stage obey the rules of society not through blind conformity but because they can understand the rational basis of these rules. Perhaps this is what is meant in the New Testament when it speaks of "being free of the law" and "a more perfect way."

Parents and teachers must feel the love of God themselves in order to "teach" their children to love God and to love others. This love is the basis of the rational-altruistic personality. The "teaching" of love is not primarily teaching with words, but teaching by visible emotional actions of love displayed by parents, teachers, and all professing Christians toward others. These actions spring from the knowledge and the assurance of God's love toward man.

EIGHT

ANXIETY AND UNCONSCIOUS
MOTIVATION

"For I do not do the good I want, but the evil I do not want is what I do." (Rom. 7:19.) This statement is recognition, twenty centuries ago, of a persistent human problem. This problem was given recognition in more modern times by psychoanalysts. We examine it in social psychology because its source is in the personal interactions of the individual with other people, and every member involved in the interactions is affected by it.

Part of the subconscious comes from the very process of internalizing social rules and regulations. We may make some of these rules so much a part of self that we no longer realize that we obey them. When the occasion arises, we act as we have been taught without giving our actions a second thought. If asked why we act in this certain way, all we can answer is, "That is the proper way to act in these circumstances." We are unable to give a rational or historic answer.

Difficulties arise when we have been taught two conflicting ways of reacting to the same situation. In our society social reward is given for getting along with others. Members of society punish us if we are hostile or aggressive by ceasing to interact with us, and this presents a possible conflict situation. As discussed in the previous chapter, an individual perceives others as threatening, and he must respond to this in some way. He knows that if he uses an attack response he will be punished by society. How can an individual resolve this conflict? Or even more basically, what in an individual makes him wish to resolve a conflict?

Conflict arouses unpleasant emotions in an individual. The emotion may be anger if the individual seeks to attack his source of frustration. It may be fear if he is threatened with damage to self-image. Fear is a very unpleasant emotion. It is one we try to avoid and, when it occurs, we try to do something immediately to relieve it. The emotion that results from internal conflict is akin to fear, but it is not quite the same. It has a familiar name, anxiety. Psychologists distinguish between fear and anxiety by defining fear as having a known object or situation that threatens self and anxiety as fearlike emotion in which no known object or situation can be perceived as threatening self.

An understanding of anxiety is important because it

is a key to many seemingly irrational actions. We seek to relieve anxiety feelings because they are unpleasant. Anxiety becomes a drive which demands relief. When we take some action that relieves anxiety, we are likely to repeat this anxiety-relieving action. The model for learning a motive presented earlier is applicable here.

need or drive+action or situation which satisfies
need=motive

anxiety+action or situation which relieves
anxiety=relief

Here we have a motive based upon anxiety. As anxiety becomes more intense, the need to escape it becomes more necessary. The motive becomes stronger.

For an individual anxiety is difficult to relieve because the sources are hidden. They are the hidden or half-hidden rules and regulations which were internalized during childhood. Anxiety is particularly intense and difficult to deal with when these rules and regulations were learned through threats to self. Each time the rule is perceived, the fear emotions associated with the rule are present.

Another source of anxiety is in the very nature of man. Man is mortal and he knows it. The products of man's civilization, its buildings, tools, language, and even its way of life seem mortal. We are reminded of this each time we see pictures of ancient Greece, Egypt, or Babylonia. There is a basic anxiety which comes to man when he realizes his finiteness or mortality. The way of life, the language, the values of a culture are part of each individual in the culture and are the source of meaning of life and man's ties with his friends. When man realizes that these may pass away or are passing away, he loses part of the meaning of life and part of the feeling of oneness with his friends. This leads to a loneliness or estrangement and a strong threat to self. The very "I am" is threatened. Man tries to alleviate this basic anxiety through assuring the survival of the values of his group or nation or civilization. Since these values are in the basic core of self, he is in essence trying to protect self.

There is anxiety in our nation today because the changes which are occurring are threatening the very values we are trying to continue. We are faced with anxiety as individuals because the values which seemed changeless are threatened by change. These values are not "out in the world" but are a vital part of each of us. They give meaning to life and tie us to our friends. Change in values, or threat of change, causes anxiety because it threatens us with meaninglessness and breaks our ties with our friends and thus causes loneliness.

In *The Lonely Crowd,* David Riesman has noted another source of anxiety, one which derives from too great insistence by parents and teachers on smooth interpersonal relations. The individual is made to feel worthless if he cannot "cooperate." To relieve the anxiety born of threat to self when he does not feel he is "getting along with others," the individual attempts to be certain of his acceptance by others. He conforms to rules and regulations of whatever groups in which he finds himself. But he can never be certain of his acceptance by others because his only evidence of acceptance is the behavior of others. He must judge whether another's behavior indicates acceptance or rejection. There is always an element of uncertainty in judging behavior. There is the nagging uncertainty, "I may be wrong." The individual is taught that he must be accepted by others, but he can never be certain of their acceptance. This results in a recurring feeling of rejection or loneliness. A person may be in a group and feel lonely. Loneliness here is part of, and results in, threat to self-image and anxiety.

There are many ways of relieving anxiety. One of these is by distorting our perception of the world. If we see our world differently, we may prevent anxiety from occurring. But how can perception be distorted? Is not perception like a photograph that shows every detail? Earlier it was mentioned that perception is the result of the stimulation of our sense organs plus the meaning that we learn to make of this pattern of sense data. It is in this interpretation of meaning that the distortion occurs. For example, three persons standing together at the time of an accident may give substantially different versions of the accident. They perceived the accident from the background of their past experiences and as a result saw somewhat different events.

We perceive the world as we have learned to perceive it. Since most of us in the same society have learned the same things, we perceive much the same. Some persons, however, because it relieves their anxiety feelings see the world differently than most people do. For example, some individuals perceive the world through "rose-colored glasses." They have learned to alleviate anxiety by perceiving a world where there is little or no danger. In a sense they deny there is danger. They do not perceive it; therefore, they have no threat to self and no anxiety.

Other individuals seek to relieve the anxiety that comes from conflict by forcing a rigid order upon their world. They limit it to those situations with which they can cope. They may try to force others to accept this limited world. This, of course, leads to difficulties in interpersonal relations because not everyone wishes to live so. For example, they may limit their world to their dwelling place and expect others to bring them the necessities of life. Another way of limiting is to adopt from a group its values, standards, and way of life and refuse to admit that any other way of life has any value. These individuals act as if their group has all of the answers to all problems and teaches the only moral way of life. Some small communities, small religious groups, or churches may be found that illustrate this way of dealing with anxiety. In a sense these persons are saying, "My community has the only correct and moral way of life. Any other way is immoral." As long as an individual is able to stay within this group, there are few conflicts and little anxiety for him because the group has answered all the questions.

We may relieve our anxieties by withdrawing into a

fantasy or dream world. In our fantasies we can construct a world free of anxiety. If other people threaten us, we can overcome this by imagining we are more powerful than they. Or we can construct a pleasant dream world where there are no conflict situations. This is not to imply that all fantasy or daydreaming is withdrawal. There are constructive aspects of fantasy as well as destructive.

The various ways of dealing with anxiety can be conscious or unconscious. We may decide to limit our group. We may say to ourselves, "For the time being it is best for me to limit my activities to those prescribed by this group. If I do not, I may suffer irreparable damage." This voluntary limiting of one's scope of action is called *suppression*. This is a conscious way of dealing with anxiety.

Anxiety may be relieved in ways which are not conscious. They are hidden from us. Our perceptions may become distorted without our conscious knowledge. We may severely limit our world of action without being at all conscious of what we are doing. This unconscious means of dealing with anxiety is called *repression*.

The way we attempt to solve our conflicts has implications for many areas of living. Rational problem-solving is a conscious attempt to overcome barriers which block goalward progress. Suppression may mean that we still want the goal but it is unattainable at the present or even at a future time. We consciously know this, but suppress our wishing and frustration and the anxiety that comes from a blocked goal. Suppression does not remove barriers to goal progress. It does not solve the problem. Repression is not a method of problem-solving at all. We repress to alleviate the anxiety created by a barrier to goalward progress. The barrier itself is perceived as ego-threatening, and this creates anxiety. We adopt a new goal of relieving our anxiety feelings. We do not try to solve the conflict. Even though we succeed in pushing a conflict into the subconscious, the conflict has not been solved.

Methods of handling conflicts and anxiety-producing situations have implications for freedom of choice. The individual who attempts to solve his problem rationally is exercising free choice. The individual who suppresses is voluntarily abrogating his freedom of choice in a situation for a period of time. He is reserving the right, however, of returning to the situation and choosing again. The individual who represses has little or no freedom of choice in the situation concerned with the repression. His actions are dictated by unconscious actions learned because they reduce his intense anxiety feelings. Thus a man may live in a "free society" and yet may not be free.

There are implications for interpersonal relations in the manner in which individuals attempt to solve conflict situations. Earlier it was said that conflicts have their origins in interpersonal relations. Those who rationally solve conflicts are being successful in interpersonal relations. They are able to use rational methods, in part, because they perceive little threat to self in their interpersonal conflicts. They see these conflicts as problems to be solved, not as egos to be defended. Because they perceive little threat from others, they do not take hostile, aggressive, or defensive actions against others. Since others perceive that there is no hostility, they are less likely to respond with hostility. Paul's thirteenth chapter of I Corinthians is a superb illustration of the perception of others' actions as nonthreatening to one's self.

In suppression and repression the interpersonal conflict is not solved. One who is suppressing voluntarily ceases to communicate with others in the area of conflict. If this is an important area, it may result in a considerable decrease or change in communication. One who is repressing has not and cannot solve the conflict because he can no longer communicate about it. He may react with feelings of great threat in areas where threat is no longer present. One cannot communicate to him the fact that threat has ceased to exist because he is unable to recognize that this is an area of threat to himself.

Why do some persons develop severe repressions and others do not? The answer is in the severity of threat to self perceived in learning the important rules and regulations of a society. If severe self-threat was used to teach these rules and regulations, the emotional feelings of threat will be learned as an integral part of the rules and regulations. Every time a rule is broken, or even the contemplating of breaking it, severe feelings of threat will be created. Under these conditions repression is likely to occur.

This does not imply that rules and regulations are not to be taught. They must be taught if one is to have a well-defined self and be a constructive member of a group. It is the manner of teaching which is important. In any teaching of the laws of society the worth of the individual in the eyes of God ought to be a constant concern. The laws must be taught, but a love for the individual ought to permeate the teaching, a love which flows from a feeling of the assurance of God's love toward all and manifests itself in a teaching process which does not threaten the integrity of self.

NINE

WE LEARN THROUGH GROUPS

One of the striking features of human life is the amount of cooperation among human beings. It might be said that the quality which defines us as humans, as different from animals, is the result of group life. From groups motives and attitudes are learned. A group enables an individual to see himself as different from others and thus develop a sense of self. The wide varieties of behavior among humans that are the result of roles are learned in the group. The looking upward, the searching for those things we ought to do, and the goals toward which we strive are learned, at least in part, from the groups of which we are members.

When the psychologist uses the term "group," he means something different from the word as used by a layman. The layman will speak of the people thrown together in a given minute of time in an elevator as a group. Perhaps a better term for this would be an "aggregate" or collection of people. In order for a psychologist to call two or more persons a group there must be certain relationships between these persons. They must have communication in which there is a sharing of attitudes, meaning, values, and goals. While these people are together, there must be an interdependence such that the role that one person plays helps to define the role or roles of others and vice versa. Henceforth, when the term "group" is used, it will imply both the sharing of attitudes, goals, and the like and the interdependence of roles.

THE GROUP TEACHES MOTIVES, ATTITUDES, ROLES, VALUES, AND GOALS

In order for persons to communicate effectively they must share the meanings of words. If one person talks about the word "table" and means a flat surface supported on four legs, and the man to whom he is talking thinks of a table only as columns of numbers in a book, there is likely to be difficulty in communication. A person to become a member of a group must learn to share the meanings of the words used in the group. As with words there must be a sharing of attitudes. Could you imagine a religious group in which some of the members had positive attitudes toward the church while other members felt the church was foisted upon people by a group of men trying to preserve an outmoded tradition? In such a group the communications would be difficult. In order to belong to a group one must share some of the major attitudes of the group.

When roles are spoken of, names of roles are used. There are many activities, attitudes, and goals which are implied in the single role-label "minister." In order to communicate in a group a person must learn what activities, attitudes, and values are implied when the role-label is used. There would be difficulty in a religious group if some persons thought of a minister as preaching, visiting, and seeking to bring persons into the church, and others thought of him as the man who ministered to them by giving them medicine when they were ill.

Members of groups not only learn about the roles in the group, they may on occasion be called to take these roles. For example, a member of a church learns through association what the role of a Sunday school superintendent involves. Later he takes this role. He learned through communication the duties of the role, and this made it possible for him to take it.

The taking of roles demands the acceptance of certain sets of attitudes and values. The educational director of a church is expected to have specified attitudes toward his church, his religion, and the people with whom he works. He is also expected to have the values which are involved in any church-related occupation. How did the educational director learn the specified roles, attitudes, and values? He learned from communication in religious groups and the family group of which he was a member. The taking of a role in any organization involves the knowledge of the duties of that role as gained through communication with group members in that organization.

There is another aspect of the learning of roles, attitudes, and values from groups which is of importance. After a man has learned a role, specified attitudes and values, and has taken that role in an organization, he does more than act it out like an actor reciting and acting the role in a play. The man begins to internalize the role and its attitudes and values. This role becomes, not something imposed by others, but the man himself when he is with the organization. He makes the duties of the role a part of himself. If he talked to himself about the role and its attitudes and values, he would say, "This is the way that men in this role ought to act. Men in this role ought to uphold these attitudes and values." The role becomes part of his self-picture and is as much a part of him as a hand or an arm or eye.

There is, of course, a continuity in personality. Our friends do not change observably from day to day or even from year to year. They do not change completely when they move from one role to another. However, there is a qualification to this. In a sense we are as many different people as there are different groups in which we move. To some extent our personalities are molded by the groups of which we are a member. When a person moves into a new group and becomes a member of it, he takes on the role and its related attitudes and values. Since we like to join groups which have attitudes, values, and goals something like ours, the change in personality is not too great. However, there are instances where changes in attitudes and values are of crucial interest to religious workers. People join groups which take them away from the values of their religion. They change their attitudes and values to that of the new group. They change because to belong to a new group they must communicate with the group members, using their words and attitudes to talk about the group's values and goals. If they remain a member of this group for a period of time the new attitudes, values, and goals become their attitudes, values, and goals.

Groups have another important function in regard to attitudes and values. As long as a person remains in the same group and the group is important to him, he is likely to maintain the same attitudes and values. Groups help to support these. Stories are told of the young man who goes away to college or into the armed forces and comes back much changed in values and attitudes. When he left the groups from which he learned his attitudes and values, he left the support of these groups and was thus more likely to take on new values and attitudes. The same young man, had he joined groups away from home which were like those at home, would have maintained his original attitudes and values.

The attitudes and values associated with a group and a role in the group become part of the self. When something threatens to change the attitudes, values, or roles in a group, the members act with emotion toward this threat. What is actually happening is that the change threatens the very conception each individual has of

95

himself. When a man retires, he is not merely ceasing to work. The values, goals, and private history of the work group had been internalized by the man, and when these are taken away, much of the meaning of life has been removed.

GROUPS THAT ARE IMPORTANT TO LEARNING ATTITUDES AND VALUES

The first and the most important group in our lives is the primary group called the family. The members of this group teach the individual his attitudes toward other people, his attitudes toward himself, his motives, values, goals, and paths to goals. Many psychiatrists and psychologists believe that the early childhood years largely determine the subsequent personality.

The family group is nonspecific in its teaching. That is to say, it teaches attitudes, values, and roles that affect all areas of life. If there is any one center where all the groups and group roles are brought to a focus in our life it is the family. The family teaches the general lessons that are necessary for living with other human beings. These lessons include attitudes toward others such as seeing others as threatening or as a source of satisfying needs, habits of interpersonal relations, the values and attitudes of the culture or nation of which we are members, the goals which are thought important in the culture and the acceptable routes to these goals, and roles such as masculine-feminine, husband-wife, child, and more specific roles which border upon vocational roles. It is no wonder that psychiatrists and psychologists place so much emphasis on the early years in the family. It is a wonder that the churches place so little time and emphasis upon this most important group.

The family has another important function as a group. It is the family which selects the out-of-family groups the child is permitted to enter. The family generally selects groups in which attitudes and values like its own are supported; thus it teaches the attitudes and values and then makes certain of their support by selecting groups for the children which continue these values. The church is one of the groups which is selected by many families.

The family selects these groups in many ways. It chooses a neighborhood in which to live. Within the neighborhood the family decides who are the "good" children to play with and who are not "good." Until the child leaves the neighborhood to enter high school, the family may exert considerable control over the groups which the child is permitted to enter. Even in high school and college the family may continue to attempt its direct control by moral persuasion, providing home facilities for recreation, permitting attendance at functions where certain groups are and prohibiting attendance at other functions, and by selecting the college the adolescent is to attend. Why children and adolescents choose groups which deviate from parental wishes will be discussed in a later section.

Groups of children of like ages are thus formed in neighborhoods, and these overlap with playground groups at school. As the child grows into adolescence and adulthood, these friendship groups have increasing power to change or to maintain attitudes and values. They always serve to broaden the attitudes and values of an individual even though they support the family's teaching. This they do because the child, in learning attitudes and values from the family, has learned from only one source. As the individual moves in the larger world of the neighborhood, he finds variations in these attitudes and values. His friends, though they may hold the same basic attitudes and values, having learned these in a unique family reflect the uniqueness of their family. The individual makes allowances for these in order to communicate effectively in the group and thus begins to broaden his own attitudes and values.

The school provides groups whose function it is to teach the child many of the values and attitudes of the culture. In school the child increases his knowledge and breadth of values. He learns more about his nation, about his city, about cooperation with others, about other nations, as well as the traditional subjects. He also begins to learn how he and his family are regarded by others. In general, the school serves to reinforce most of the attitudes and values of the family, especially if this family is in the middle class.

The school situation also serves to broaden the attitudes and values of children because they come into contact with more and more children with attitudes and values different from theirs. This is especially true in the American high school. The large American high school has representatives of different social classes, nationalities, and cultural subgroups. The individual may meet persons whose attitudes and values are in conflict with his, so that he is forced to think through his attitude and value system and perhaps modify it.

The group with whom an adult works serves to modify the attitudes and values of the individual. Many hours a week are spent with one group of people. Since communication with these people is necessary, the person may modify his attitudes and values by taking on the values of those around him.

The group in which most of us are interested has been reserved for discussion at this point. What about the church as a group? Undoubtedly the church serves as an important, close-knit group for some people. The church as a group for most persons is not very important. A specific church is, for many, a collection of somewhat like-minded persons rather than a group whose roles, attitudes, and values are widely shared. The day of the neighborhood churches is passing, especially in urban areas. A neighborhood, with its church, was once a unity. Neighborhoods today are seldom unified, especially in regard to churches. With modern transportation it is possible to travel some distance to churches, and this is being done. It is fairly easy to find urban churches who have scarcely a member in the immediate neighborhood. Since the members of these churches may see each other only on Sunday, the effect of church groups upon these people is negligible. However, the church may be very effective as it works through the most important of all groups, the family.

In discussing the problems of a local church as a group, perhaps it would be well to discuss why people join groups, including churches.

WHY WE CHOOSE ONE GROUP RATHER THAN ANOTHER

Groups serve to satisfy needs, and this is one of the reasons for joining. Human beings like to be and have a learned need to be around other human beings. But why choose a certain group? Parents teach their children attitudes, values, and goals. Some of the groups parents introduce children into are liked by the children because they fulfill the need induced by the teaching of the parents. When adults join groups, they do so because of the needs taught by their parents and by other socializing groups such as the school. The need that is being satisfied by the group is not always known to the individual himself. In fact, he may never stop to analyze why one group seems to be his and another always seems to be strange to him. By studying individuals the psychologists may be able to explain the motivation of the individual to choose a certain group.

There are many and complex reasons why individuals join groups. One of the obvious reasons is that a person likes the goals of a group and joins to aid the group, and himself, in reaching these goals. There are service organizations in the community which attract individuals because they offer goals to be worked for.

Another reason is the need to minimize conflict situations. This may be done by selecting groups with similar attitudes and values. In a previous chapter the source of anxiety in interpersonal conflict was analyzed. Individuals have a need to move away from sources of conflict and the resulting anxiety toward less stressful situations. We chose as friends those persons who have attitudes and values like our own because there is little conflict with them. We join groups whose members are like ourselves in order to minimize the interpersonal conflict and anxiety which comes from divergent attitudes and values. One research study showed that groups of friends at the end of four years of college were very similar in attitudes and values. The members of these groups were similar the first day of college even though they were not yet acquainted with one another. In other words, individuals of like attitudes and values choose one another.

Some groups are joined because the individual approves of the values of the group and wishes to help maintain these values. Many church members are in churches for this reason. These individuals see the church's goal as that of maintaining certain goals which they as individuals wish to perpetuate.

Prestige is another reason for joining a group. The church enjoys a certain prestige in our culture, and this attracts some people to it. One particular denomination may have a higher prestige than another. In several research studies it has been determined that the denominations may be ranked as to the socio-economic group which constitutes its membership. If an individual sees a church of a certain denomination as incorporating the prestige of a desired social class, he may join to enjoy this prestige. Some persons join a group to be with individuals whom they perceive as having high prestige in the community. Joining the group is a way of being a part of this higher prestige.

Some people join groups in order to be with their friends. When we enjoy being with certain people, we seek to make our associations with them often and long-lasting. If our friends recommend a group, or we feel we can enjoy their company more often by joining a group, we affiliate ourselves with it.

Above are listed some of the many reasons why individuals join groups. Only one of the reasons is directly concerned with goals. Does this indicate that most members of groups are not concerned with the goals of the group? This depends upon who defines what the group's goals are. What are the goals of the various groups that make up our local churches? What are the goals of the Sunday school class, board of stewards or deacons, women's mission groups, laymen's organizations, and the church softball team? The local church serves a need for the individual. This need may or may not be related to the official goals of the church. These members who are in the church for reasons other than the official goals of the church may not support—in fact, may oppose—the attempt of the church to move toward its official goals. The welding together of individuals into a group with common ideals and goals will be treated in a later chapter.

SPECIALIZATION IN MODERN LIFE AND ITS EFFECTS UPON THE CHURCH

In the agricultural community which is our heritage the number of groups in which a person participated was much fewer than in modern life. The family group and the work group were almost the same. The church group was made up of family groups living in the same community. The groups were interrelated not only through the church but through social activities and cooperative work ventures. Even in the cities at this time there was a great overlap in groups. Although for many men the work group was distinct from the family, there was some overlap because often those who worked in the same factory or business lived near one another. The churches served neighborhoods which were somewhat homogeneous in social class. A church might even serve as a point of integration for the groups in the immediate neighborhood.

The rural society has been largely displaced by the modern specialized society. Just as we have specialization in occupations, so have we specialized the groups that make up the society. The family group scarcely overlaps the work group. The family groups who make up the local church may have little or no contact with one another except in the church situation. The large, modern, grade school or high school represents not one community but many communities and calls for its own specialized service groups. Social groups may or may not overlap with work or church groups. Service groups for men or women draw their participants from many sections of the city and are likely not to overlap with any other groups. The number of groups of which an individual must be a member have multiplied: family group, work group, professional organization, service group, Parent-Teacher Association, women's clubs, Rotary, Lions, lodge, bridge club, church groups, and on and on. Each of these groups asks some measure of loyalty. Each deals with a different sphere of action. Each demands that a life be divided into different areas —family, work-social, church, church-social, service, school, and so forth. Where is the integrating factor in such a life? In the rural community the integrating factor was often the church. Today the church is, for many, another group to join.

In each of these groups the individual participating must learn the prescribed role, the attitudes, and values in order to communicate in the group. If a group is important to the individual because of the amount of time he spends in it and the number of his needs it satisfies, the role, attitudes, and values of this group may take precedence over the roles, attitudes, and values of other groups. The one most likely to satisfy the needs for long periods of time is the work group.

For many individuals the groups in which they participate present conflicting demands. Groups require that we spend our time in meetings, and inevitably two groups will schedule meetings at the same time. Or, having spent our time with one group, we feel we do not have time for another group. However, time is not the only source of conflict. One group may require roles, attitudes, and values that conflict with those of another group. One way of resolving these conflicts is to reserve areas of influence for the many groups of which one is a member. The work group and its values and attitudes are dominant in the work sphere, and no other group may interfere. The social group is confined to social affairs. The church group is concerned with Sunday and religious affairs, but it must not interfere with the work group or the social group. To speak figuratively, the individual builds a wall around each of his groups so that the conflicts that might arise are prevented from happening. The complaint often heard from this individual is, "The church has no business meddling in the methods of business." The church with its demands for integration of life around religious principles meets instant resistance from persons of this type. For them to try to integrate their life around religious teaching would be to open up all the conflicts which have been so carefully walled in.

WHY ARE THE ROLES, ATTITUDES, AND VALUES OF ONE GROUP DOMINANT OVER OTHER GROUPS?

Earlier it was said that individuals join groups to satisfy their needs. Some of the groups in which one participates provide more need satisfaction than other groups. Thus the work group may provide for the satisfaction of economic, social, and prestige needs. A group that provides a meeting each day for many hours of the day has the opportunity for satisfying more needs than a group that meets only once a week or month. A group that meets often is more likely to increase its power to satisfy needs by teaching the individuals the values and attitudes of the group. The members of the group internalize the attitudes and values and treat them as if they were to be upheld and worked for by the individuals. The individual can work for these attitudes and values through the group. This is a circle. The group teaches needs which can only be satisfied by that group.

The individual who is just entering the work world may have rather diffuse and undefined needs for status and prestige. This individual will define prestige in terms of the needs of the organization which he joins. The young man learns that to have prestige in this organization you must participate in certain rituals like cocktail parties, wear certain kinds of suits, and work by certain prescribed routes to obtain status positions such as superviser, junior executive, executive, vice-president and president. The need for prestige and status was present before the job was taken, but the organization gave it definition.

A business organization may demand, in subtle ways of course, that the rising young man pattern his total life around the values and attitudes defined by the organization. It may require the wife and family to conform to its values, attitudes, and actional system. Numerous articles in magazines have described the selection procedure certain businesses use for their executives. Certainly any young man wishing to rise in the business world will read the demands of these groups and give them serious thought. An excellent portrayal of these demands is given in the book, *The Organization Man,* by William H. Whyte.

What is the church to do in this day of many groups, each with its demands of loyalty and time? One of the solutions is to make the groups within the church stronger and more effective in their appeals. This is the subject of the next chapter.

TEN

BUILDING GROUP SOLIDARITY

Throughout the New Testament the importance of groups in the lives of the men and women who are portrayed there may be noted. The disciples formed a group. After Pentecost the churches appeared as small groups. The Epistles of Paul may be seen as communications designed both to establish the correct attitudes, values, and goals and to increase the solidarity of the groups. This is the constant task of the church, to establish fellowships of believers in furtherance of the kingdom of God. The attractions of the many groups in modern life increase the difficulties of developing cohesive, effective church groups. Perhaps a deliberate analysis of the problems involved and a utilization of principles of social psychology may aid in developing cohesive groups.

108

GROUPS MEET NEEDS

As has been stated previously, groups are joined because they meet the needs of individuals. Certainly any one group satisfies more than one need. Every group satisfies the universal need of being with other people. Other needs such as contact with members of the opposite sex, hunger, security, prestige, achievement, and integration of life values are satisfied in groups. Some groups satisfy more needs than others. To some extent the group that satisfies more needs than another group will be preferred.

One of the needs that each individual brings to his group is the need for satisfying interpersonal relationships. No one wishes to be a member of a group which is in a constant state of internal conflict. Groups are chosen partly on the basis of personal liking for the members of the group. This personal liking may depend upon how much alike the members are in attitudes and values.

What needs do the groups within a church meet? Certainly if the church is to act as an integrating force in our society it must meet a wide range of needs. It must meet these in a way that is both satisfying to the individual and within the scope of the values and goals of the church. It must meet these needs in such a way that it serves as an integrating force. Many times it seems as if the groups meeting under the auspices of the church are going off in all directions. They meet under the roof of the church building, but their activities are

109

not seen as being related to the major values and goals of the church.

MEMBERS OF A GROUP MUST SHARE GOALS, ATTITUDES, AND VALUES

The members of a church are representatives of many diverse groups within the community, and as such they may represent diverse attitudes, values, and goals. In order for the groups within the church to have strong cohesiveness the members must share a common body of attitudes, values, and goals. It is true that in the American culture there are common expectations of what the goals, attitudes, and values of the church are. It is somewhat doubtful that these expectations are always correct. In any case they may be so weak as to contribute little toward unity. They may, in fact, contribute to disunity, since members of the group may have conflicts about the correct attitudes, values, and goals.

In order for a group to be cohesive there must be a sharing of—consensus of opinion about—the values, attitudes, goals, and roles in the group. This sharing occurs only through communication. In order for church groups to develop these shared ideas they must meet often enough to communicate. The developing of shared attitudes, values, and goals occurs only when each member can learn the opinions of the other members, test his opinions against those of the other members and especially against the official opinions of the church. If these groups do not meet often, the sharing of attitudes, values, and goals will be only on a superficial level.

110

Sharing attitudes and values is more than just listening. Too often in our church groups we sit and listen but do not share our opinions, hopes, and needs. In order for there to be a sharing of attitudes and values, each person must talk and each must listen.

COMMUNICATION AND THE DEFINITION OF SOCIAL REALITY

It is not difficult to learn the boundaries and many of the features of our physical world. Concrete walls refuse to move when we walk into them. Chairs usually support us when we sit in them. The physical world remains stable and thus enables us to define its limits or its reality. The same is not true of our social world. As was discussed in a previous section, the boundaries of our social world are defined by the people around us. The reality of our social rules is established by the constancy of action of the persons upholding the social rules. For us the reality of our moral order is established by the constancy of those who uphold this order. The manner in which these rules are held constant is by communication. We are told when we transgress. We hear talk of the variations of the rules, of when a rule pertains and when it does not. We know a rule is real because we see it in the actions of others and hear about it in their conversation. We can test it for ourselves if we wish. What is the reality of patriotism? What is the reality of the love of God if it is not expressed in interpersonal relations such as communications? We need some test of

111

the reality of our religious experience. This test is possible through our communication with others who are having similar experiences. There is a reality of our experience with God himself, but this reality is deepened and made more meaningful as we share it with others who have had experience with God. This is a sharing of experiences with like-minded people.

What is the result when the group members do not share their religious experience? Part of the reality of this experience is lost. A member of the group might say to himself, "I thought my religious experience was genuine, but no one in my group has reported such an experience as mine. Therefore, I must be mistaken." It is in the sharing of these experiences that the members of groups test the reality of the religious experience. In I Sam. 3:3-10 is told the story of Samuel's call from God. Samuel found it necessary to go to Eli to test the reality of this call.

TO BE COHESIVE A GROUP MUST BE ABLE TO DISTINGUISH ITSELF FROM OTHER GROUPS

Some groups in order to distinguish themselves from other groups use a special uniform. Ezra initiated strict adherence to Jewish law in order to mark the differences between Jewish and Gentile groups. The early Christian church used various symbols to distinguish their group from others. What is the mark of the modern religious group? What distinguishes the Christian or Jewish group from any other? This is a pertinent question to ask in this age. A great part of the Judeo-Christian tradition has been incorporated into the culture pattern of the Western world. This makes it possible for a group outside the church to have as part of its official attitudes those values and goals which are elements of the Judeo-Christian belief. Individuals may find it difficult to hold strong loyalty to a group that is practically indistinguishable from other groups. In order for the members of church groups to develop a loyalty to the church they must have something to be loyal to which distinguishes their group from others. What is the mark of the religious group? The attitudes, values, and goals of the religious group must be emphasized and incorporated as part of the shared beliefs of the group, and those which distinguish the religious group from others need special emphasis. This, of course, requires the leadership of those who know the marks of their religious beliefs.

THE SHARING OF PROGRESS TOWARD GOALS

There have been many church groups which have enjoyed the fellowship of working together to build the church from a few members to many and to construct the buildings from the ground up, only to see the fellowship of the members of the church crumble in conflict when the building was finished. This is an example of the effect of sharing in a task or goal. During the building of the church the goal was obvious, and individuals were able to contribute their talents to it. They could see what needed to be done. When the church building was completed and paid for, there was no visible goal.

113

The members of a group, to feel a strong sense of unity, need to involve themselves in a group goal. Each member needs to feel that the goal of the group is his goal; that when the group achieves, he achieves; when he achieves, the group benefits. This is possible as long as there is a well-defined goal toward which the group is making visible progress. When the group no longer has a goal, its reason for being is lost, and there is a resulting loss of cohesion. The members no longer have anything to share.

The church has more difficulty establishing goals than do organizations which are dedicated to reaching goals which are short-range and easily seen. Our religious goals are to seek changes in attitudes, in the way we perceive others, in our actions. It is much more difficult to challenge people to reach for "invisible" goals such as changed values than to reach goals as visible as a brick building. But it is from, and to, the glory of the kingdom of God that some men have challenged others to such "invisible" goals.

Though the community of believers of this generation is at one with the community of all generations, it is unique in that its problems are different from those of the community of believers who lived in past generations. The Old and New Testaments are records of new challenges met and new goals set. Problems change, and with them the goals of solving these problems. Group goals must challenge the members of the group. The leaders of these groups are the members who perceive these new problems and challenge others to make the solution of these problems the goals of the group.

What are the goals of the church groups? Goals must be set which distinguish them from nonchurch groups and toward which they may maintain progress. The process of goal-setting falls to the leadership of the group.

WHAT IS THE EFFECT OF THE SIZE OF THE GROUP?

There is a tendency toward large churches in modern America. The large church has a prestige both for members and pastor that the small church does not. However, the large church has disadvantages that are not faced by the small church. These disadvantages are in the nature of the church as an effective group for the members of the church. Can the large church have a sharing of beliefs and religious experiences throughout its membership? Can the large church serve as a group attractive enough to draw the consuming loyalty of the members of other urban groups? The answers must be that the large church cannot hope to be a unified cohesive group. Only small churches can hope to achieve this.

If the church is to be a unifying or integrating force in the lives of individuals in modern urban America, it must solve the problems concerning group loyalty, cohesiveness, and goals. One way to do this would be to divide each church into smaller churches. There are disadvantages to this, and it is not conceivable that such an action would be taken. What then can be done if the church as a whole cannot be a group? There must be groups constituted within a local church which meet the following requirements. They must be small enough to allow communication between members. They must provide for frequent enough meetings so that a sharing of attitudes, values, and goals is achieved. The sharing of beliefs mentioned in the previous paragraph must occur to the extent that it leads to the sharing of religious experiences. The groups must have goals which are shared by the members and which are goals of the church itself. The goals and experiences within the groups must be of such a nature that they not only satisfy the needs of the members but also enable the members to distinguish themselves and their group from nonchurch groups.

Sunday school classes are constituted groups within the church and with guidance may fit themselves into the above requirements. It may be possible for the class or elements of the class to meet at times throughout the week to share experiences and work for the goals of the group. Leadership of the class in terms of goal setting, setting and maintaining attitudes and values different from nonchurch groups yet consistent with the tradition of the church, may be provided by the Sunday school teacher. There are obvious disadvantages to the use of Sunday school classes to provide the necessary small groups within a large church. The members of the class may live in different parts of the city and not be in contact with one another during the week. The leadership may be uneducated in the goals of the church, or not in sympathy with them, and thus not guide the class toward these goals. Last but not least, the class may develop into a clique which feels itself independent of the church and not completely in sympathy with the attitudes, values, and goals of the church.

Another suggestion that has been made is the creation of house-churches. Within a church a certain outstanding person would be trained to work with a group whose members live near him. The home becomes the church. There are disadvantages to this also. Though the members of the group live close enough to meet often, they may form a clique whose beliefs are at variance with the church itself. As with the Sunday school class, the crucial person is the teacher or the leader of the group, just as the pastor is crucial within the church.

The most important group through which the church may work is already constituted, generally has strong loyalties, cohesion, and in most cases the practice of sharing beliefs. This group is the family. It is not the solution to the entire problem, but more emphasis on the family as a part of the teaching and worship function of the church would certainly do much to alleviate the problem. To make a bold statement—it might be said that the church is only effective inasmuch as it affects the families within it.

THE LEADER AND THE GROUP

Leadership is commonly thought of as traits possessed by certain individuals but not by others. If one possesses these traits he is a leader. If he does not possess them he cannot become a leader. There has been considerable research on the problem of leadership since World War II. One of the first findings of this research was that there were no traits that distinguished leaders from nonleaders. In a review of the literature of research studies done on the problem of leadership during and before World War II it was determined that the researchers contradicted one another. One study would find that one trait marked the difference between leaders and nonleaders. Another would find that this trait was not important in telling the differences. More recent studies have confirmed the conclusion that the solution to the problem of "What is leadership?" is not to be found in traits of the individual leader.

Another of the older ideas of leadership was that a leader in one situation would be a good leader in another situation. Except for one factor this conclusion has not been confirmed by modern research. That one factor is the transfer of prestige from one situation to another. The man who is a successful president of a large company is likely to be chosen as the leader of other groups. When he assumes leadership, his prestige as president of this company may cause many in the new group to pay the same deference to him as his employees do.

There is one quality which leaders must have, skill in interpersonal relations. This, however, is a skill that characterizes many nonleaders as well as leaders.

A reason why many psychologists and sociologists

working in research in leadership have dropped the notion of specific leader traits has been that in observing leaders and their groups in action they have noted shifts in leadership. The appointed leader is not always the leader of the group during action by the group. As the demands of the situation shift, the leadership shifts to other members of the group. Leadership then is a function of the group.

The more recent views on leadership stress that the leadership is an integral part of the group and cannot be understood apart from the group. The role of the leader is one of the roles in the group. As such it is defined by the other roles and interlocks with all the roles in the group. Leadership is discussed in this book in the section about groups because the leader and the group cannot be separated. A complete discussion of the problems of leadership would take a book in itself. Here we will confine ourselves to discussing the effect of the leader or the duties of the leader as they pertain to the cohesiveness of the group, the goals set by the group, and the maintenance of the attitudes, values, and goals of the groups. We seek to elaborate upon the functions of leadership mentioned only in passing in the previous section.

THE LEADER FACILITATES GROUP ACTION AND THE SHARING OF BELIEFS

The leader, as a member of the group, shares the attitudes, values, and goals of the group. In fact, it might be said that he epitomizes them. The leader aids in the sharing of the group's beliefs. He may do this by acting as mediator when there are controversies about group beliefs. On other occasions he accomplishes it by being the judge of the correctness of views. Though he may act to change the views of the group, he must always do this through a gradual sharing of new attitudes, values, and goals. The function of facilitator is vital and crucial in church groups. Not only does the leader facilitate the sharing of attitudes, values, and goals, he must be in a position to judge the correctness of these. Groups within churches can be found which have shared values or goals that are at some variance with the stated values and goals of the church. In providing proper trained leadership the church insures that the beliefs of the groups in the church are not at variance with the stated beliefs of the church.

In helping the group to understand and share the proper attitudes, beliefs, and values, the leader aids the group in defining itself as different from other groups. Certainly there are attitudes, values, and goals within Christian belief that distinguish the member of a Christian group from those who hold merely the cultural marks of Christianity. The task of the leader of the church group is to know these differences and to help the group adopt the attitudes, values, and goals as part of the group's shared beliefs. There is a danger in the process of helping a religious group differentiate itself from non-Christian groups. This danger is that they will see themselves as better than other groups or develop what is called the "holier than thou" attitude.

This is certainly not a part of the religious values system. A danger that springs from the above is the feeling that since we are different we will not let others into the group. This again is not in the Christian value system and, further, is opposed to the Christian value of evangelism.

There is a tendency on the part of some so-called leaders to dominate totally the groups they lead. They determine the correctness of the goals, attitudes, and values of the group. The only voice they tolerate within the group is the voice that supports them. Though these groups may appear to be strong, there may not be sharing within the group. Goals must be internalized by all members of the group, and all must feel a share in their support. It is difficult to feel involved in a goal not of one's choosing. Most church groups today are voluntary groups. The leader can exercise little absolute authority over the members. The group members can always say, "This is as much my group as yours, and if you don't like what we are doing, leave." As was mentioned earlier, the leader must share the beliefs of the group. If he moves too far from the group in his personal beliefs, the group will reject him. The leader of the modern church group cannot arbitrarily change the beliefs of the group. He may feel that the attitudes, values, or goals are in error, but he cannot demand their change. The only changes which he can accomplish are by working through the structure of the group. This means that the members must be involved in whatever new goals the leader sets for the group. If the leader can successfully involve the members in changes in goals, values, and attitudes, then the group will change. If the leader cannot do this, the group may disintegrate, or may reject the leader and ignore his proposals.

The goals of the church are not always popular. For this reason many church groups ignore them or give superficial support to them. One of the most difficult tasks of the religious leader is to keep the group oriented toward the goals of the church. The letters of Paul to the churches illustrate this difficulty even in the earliest days of the church. When the appointed leader and actual leadership is different, as it usually is, the appointed leader must work always through the actual leadership of the group. This does not mean that the appointed leader work only with one person, since leadership within a group may vary with the situation. The appointed leader in recognizing this may work first with one and then another member of a group. However, the appointed leader must always recognize the integrity of the group.

THE APPOINTED LEADER MAY ASSUME TOO MANY DUTIES

There are many who have been appointed to leadership positions whose motto is, "The best way to get a job done is to do it yourself." Whatever the merits of this point of view for leadership outside the church, it has no merit within the church. The goal of the church is not to get a certain report into the national or state office, or to get the nursery painted, or other similar tasks. The goal of the church is to involve people's lives with God. The leader who attempts to assume all the functions of the groups in the church is depriving them of their reason for being. If such a leader is in the church long enough, the groups wither and die. The task of the leader appointed to a church is to involve individuals in the activities, attitudes, values, and goals of groups, not to assume all activities for himself. It may be true that the leader can accomplish the task in less time, with less strain to himself, and with more accuracy than can the groups in the church, but the leader who thinks this is his function has missed the goal of the church.

Some ministers or church leaders by attempting to do everything themselves leave the church with weak groups. Other ministers and church workers leave the church stronger than they found it. They work through the established leaders and their groups, or where few exist, they build new groups. They aid these groups to become cohesive. They involve the individual members of the groups in the activities and beliefs of the church as a whole.

ELEVEN

THE CHANGING AND THE SUPPORTING OF ATTITUDES

We want some individuals to change their attitudes and values toward the teachings of Christianity. Other individuals we pray will not change. Attitudes and values are neither chiseled in living rock, nor are they shifting sand. In all of us some attitudes are changing, and some are relatively permanent. "Growing faith" is a term used to describe the change of attitudes and values toward a mature faith with an underlying permanent set of values guiding the change.

When children mature and leave home for work, the armed services, college, or to establish their homes, we hope that they will remember and follow the values they have learned from us, the local community, and the church. The amount and the direction of their

124

change depend upon many factors. What these factors are and how they work is the subject of this chapter.

Whether or not the attitude is part of the self-image affects the ease or difficulty of changing the attitude. In general, if the attitude change is perceived by the individual as enhancing his self-image, he will change. When those attitudes which are an integral part of self are challenged, there is immediate resistance because of the threat to the self-image.

Attitudes which are supported by a group in which a person is involved are more difficult to change than attitudes not supported by the group. The more one is involved in a group the less likely it is that his attitudes will change if they are of major importance to the group.

Common attitudes are necessary for communication within a group. The change of attitudes on the part of an individual member creates difficulties in communications with the group. The less one can communicate with other group members, the less he is a part of the group. To remain a member of the group an individual must continue to communicate with the other members, and to do this he must maintain attitudes important to the group.

The members of a group and the collective attitudes, values, and goals of a group become part of the self-image of each member. Attempts to change the attitudes of any one member of the group threatens him with loss of self-image from several sources. A change in attitude may threaten an individual with the loss of other members of the group who have become, in a sense, part of the self of the individual; that is, if one changes, he may be rejected by the other members. Since the group members and their collective attitudes, values, roles, and goals help give meaning to life, any separation from the group threatens one with meaninglessness.

A single attitude does not exist. We use the word "attitude" for convenience. Attitudes, as we noted in Chapter 3, are part of systems of attitudes. When we talk of attitude change, we must think of changing a system of attitudes, some of which are elaborate and widespread. A system of attitudes toward God is related to attitudes toward the church and morality; it also may be related to political, economic, and social beliefs. Other attitude systems are not at all widespread. How difficult or easy it is to change attitudes depends in part to what extent the attitudes being changed are related to other attitudes.

According to several attitude surveys which have been made, the majority of persons living in this country believe in God and belong to a religious group. The percentage of persons denying that there is a God is less than ten. Most of the efforts of workers for the church is toward strengthening present beliefs or attempting to broaden the attitude system. They are attempting to move an individual's attitudes in the direction toward which the individual believes. This is called congruent change. The individual believes in God. The religious worker wants to take this individual further in this same belief.

At times, however, we may wish to induce a person

126

to change his attitude so that he moves in the opposite direction. For example, we may wish to change an atheist's attitude from denial of God to belief in God. This is called incongruent attitude change.

The two types of attitude change are introduced because different ways of attempting to change attitudes affect people differently, depending on whether the change desired is congruent or incongruent with their present attitudes.

Generally speaking, attempts to change attitudes in the same direction, congruent, do not threaten the self. Attempts to change attitudes in the opposite direction lead to threats to self. Needless to say, congruent changes are easier to make.

If most individuals in this country believe in God, why is it so difficult to persuade people to take a more active interest in Christian work and life? It would seem that we are trying to make congruent change. However, we must perceive the total attitude systems in which belief in God is embedded in order to understand the reluctance of many individuals to take an active part in Christian life.

As was noted earlier in discussing reasons why individuals join one group rather than another, individuals may choose a group whose goals are different from theirs. They may join a club because it is the socially acceptable act or because they like the other group members, only to find that they really do not like its activities.

In our society there is a belief that the only business of the church is man's relation to God and that this relation is an act of thought or faith. Any deviation from this relation to God toward affairs of the world is resisted. The church may be thought of as an organization which works within a defined sphere of life. Other organizations have equally important spheres of action. When the church tries to move beyond its socially defined sphere of action, it is competing with other organizations. To an individual this competition means internal conflict and anxiety. Since the church seems to be the disturbing group, resistance is built up against any movement of the church into spheres of action which conflict with other groups' actions. In any case, much of the change of attitudes which we would like to persuade church members to accept are incongruent with some of their present attitudes.

METHODS OF CHANGING ATTITUDES

Let us look now at some of the methods used to change attitudes. These methods will be presented under four headings: (1) giving information or increasing knowledge; (2) increasing familiarity with the attitude object; (3) using prestige figures; (4) using mass communication methods. These methods overlap to some extent; but since they represent different efforts on the part of religious bodies, they will be treated separately. These methods may be used to strengthen and to provide support for present attitudes. They are applicable to congruent change but ineffective for incongruent change.

1. Giving information or increasing knowledge. A great deal of the effort of religious bodies is expended in teaching the history, traditions, beliefs, or doctrines of the organization. The Sunday school movement was instituted for such purposes. Some effort and expense is incurred to assure that proper teaching methods will be used. However, most church school teachers are without formal training in either their method of teaching or in their content material. If it is obvious to the pupil in church school that the teacher has put little effort into preparing the lesson, the student may develop the attitude that the material being taught is not worth very much. This, coupled with the knowledge that church school is only once a week, should encourage the youth to place little emphasis on the material taught in church school.

There are several sources of distortions that may occur in the material. The first distortion is due to the attitudes of the teacher toward the information which he is to teach. If he has mistaken and immature attitudes toward religion, he is likely to read these attitudes into the material he is to teach. He thus perpetuates his immature ideas.

The second source of distortion lies in the attitudes of the student. He accepts facts that are in accord with his attitudes. Facts not in accord with his attitudes may be changed so that they do fit or they may not be remembered. Earlier we discussed distortion in perception. That is what is occurring here. The student distorts and selects the incoming information so that it fits his attitudes. It is a mistake to think of the student as soaking up the information which is presented to him. He learns in accord with his needs and attitudes. The teacher, in presenting information, must keep in mind the needs of the age group which he is teaching. The teacher must study the pupil as much as the information. The information and attitudes which the church school teacher is attempting to teach may be in competition with the needs, goals, values, and attitudes of the students, family group, and age-mate group. The student may reject certain religious facts and attitudes because his family disapproves of them or because he would have to leave his friends if he continued to hold them.

In spite of the great limitations of the use of information and increasing knowledge to change attitudes, this method is still one of the most widespread. There are lessons to be gained from research which will aid in changing attitudes. First is a restatement of what was mentioned previously. The teacher must know the needs, motives, goals, and attitudes of his students, and the information must be presented in relation to these. This implies that the teacher listens to what the student has to say. Second, it has been found that for the person of average or above average intelligence presenting both sides of a question is best for the changing of attitudes. Certainly if the student is listening to what the teacher is saying, he will think of some questions pertaining to the other side whether the teacher mentions them or not. Depending upon his curiosity and relationship with his teacher, he may ask these questions.

If only one side of the question is taught, the student might feel that the teacher was trying to influence him, and this would result in resistance on the part of the student. Much of the information taught in church schools pertains to values and not to fact. The teacher may teach both sides of the question and still express an opinion favoring one of the viewpoints.

2. Increasing familiarity with the attitude object. It is difficult to explain situations which are outside the realm of experience of the listeners. Many situations which are taught in church schools are of this nature. How do you explain to young people the tragedy of poverty when they are not associated with it? How do you explain the necessity for medical missions to a foreign land when they have no concept of the standard of living of the other nation? The knowledge and attitudes associated with these and similar situations could be presented much better by firsthand experience or pictures than by words. Church young people can be shown poverty and its effects by taking them into such situations. Intolerance of those of different denominations or faiths can be changed by encouraging meetings of young people in which members of other faiths and denominations participate. The program of the National Conference of Christians and Jews is such an effort. Pictures of the suffering of children in Korea and Europe that appear in newspapers are more effective than mere talking about the plight of these children. The more familiar individuals are with others and their

situations, the more likely that positive attitudes will exist.

3. Using prestige figures. One of the needs that young people have learned from their culture is the need of prestige. An attempt to be like prestige figures in dress and action is apparent in the actions of many of our young people. Church school teachers and the churches as organizations point out certain prestige figures because they are church members or because they have made statements favorable to religion. Joe Jones, who is an All-American from Central University, is going to preach tonight. This is an appeal to those who believe in the prestige of the football star. Successful businessmen are called upon to speak at church. The President of the United States asks that we participate in a day of prayer. All of these take advantage of the power of prestige to bring people into the church and to change or strengthen their attitudes toward aspects of religion.

These appeals of prestige are successful with those whose attitudes are neutral or weak and who regard the person making the speech or appeal as a prestige figure. This is one type of witness for religion. The prestige suggestion is likely to be disregarded if the figure making the appeal is not perceived as a prestige figure, or if the appeal is out of character for the prestige figure.

There are dangers to prestige figures being used. What happens if the prestige figure speaking for religion later is reported to do or say something which is against the tenets of the faith? Young people are often disappointed in the actions of prestige figures. Somehow they seem to violate the very tenets which they preach. The attitudes formed from such disappointments may be opposite to the one intended by the church or church worker.

4. Using mass communications methods. Churches give much support to publications, motion pictures, radio and television programs which seek to carry the message of the church. In these methods the church may dramatize its appeal and show how religion can meet needs which are now without satisfaction. The use of motion pictures is one method to increase familiarity with situations far removed from our daily life. The various denominations have presented television series to acquaint viewers with the message of religion. The value of many of these mass communication methods, motion pictures and dramas on television in particular, cannot be denied. But there are limitations to such methods.

The effect of mass communication media is restricted to those who read it, see it, or hear it. People choose their reading material according to their interests, attitudes, and values. The literature of the church is read most widely by those already in favor of the attitudes and values of the church. People choose television and radio programs according to their needs, attitudes, and values. If they are not already predisposed toward the message of religion, they are not likely to spend time listening to it on radio or watching it on television. Again we find that those who are already predisposed toward the message of the church are the listeners and viewers. The motion pictures used by church groups are provided by the denominations and are shown in churches to church groups. It is not denied that mass communication media have an effect upon attitudes. The effect, however, is likely to be upon those already in the religious groups. The great mass of people outside formal religious groups may be largely unaffected by these methods.

SUPPORTING ATTITUDES THROUGH GROUPS

The process of making the attitudes, values, and goals of a group part of one's personality has been covered in a previous chapter. This process is vital to helping those who are new in the faith or those who have moved into the community and are joining a new church. Many individuals are lost to the church when they are new in faith or new in the community. This loss can be prevented in large measure by providing church groups into which these individuals may be absorbed. These groups are necessary because of the challenge of the many other groups in the community. Few groups in a community are antireligious; they are nonreligious, or they are nominally religious. The individuals new in faith or the community may find that these secular groups offer more satisfaction of human needs than the church group. In joining and becoming a part of these secular groups the individual learns and makes a part of self the attitudes, values, roles, and goals of these groups. To prevent this from occurring the church should provide groups in which the new in faith or new in community can find both need satisfaction and anchorage for their attitudes. These groups also provide the beginning point for continued growth in religious maturity.

One of the serious limitations of the four attitude change methods listed in the previous section is that they are one-sided. One person talks to many others. There is little opportunity for the listener to test whether or not he has understood correctly because he cannot "talk back." The back talk not only provides a way of testing the reality of the hearer's perceptions, it also gives him the opportunity of tying the new ideas into his present ideas.

Another limitation is that seldom is group support for new ideas provided. The individual listener is, in a sense, alone. This lack of group support is one of the reasons why many evangelizing programs and religious instructions at youth camps fail. Individuals seem convinced of the rightness of the information they have received. Leaders of the program seem convinced also that their attempts were successful. Two weeks or two months after the program many of those who seemed convinced have returned to their original beliefs and ways. One reason this happens is that the individual has little or no support for his changed attitudes when he returns to his home group. It might be more effective to bring functioning groups into such programs, give them a chance both to listen and to discuss among themselves. Then new information would become part of group attitudes, and support for each individual would be assured.

INCONGRUENT CHANGE

How do you change the attitudes of one who is antagonistic toward religion? How do you change the strongly held erroneous, immature attitudes of those within the fold of the church? If an attempt is made to change attitudes by providing more information to these people, one may find stronger resistance than ever. Attitudes are strongly held because they have become a part of the self-picture. These attitudes help relate the self to the outside world. When an attack is made upon these attitudes that relate the self to the outside world, the attack is seen as destroying the very supports of selfhood. No one can tolerate such an attack without defending those attitudes which are being attacked. It is for this reason that it is difficult to change strongly held attitudes.

So many of the attempts to change attitudes serve only to increase resistance to change. Attempts to overwhelm a person with information contrary to his attitudes usually results in feelings of antagonism on both sides. He feels antagonistic because you have attempted to break down his necessary defenses, and you feel antagonistic because he will not listen objectively to your arguments. When an attempt is being made to change someone's attitude and he begins to be antagonistic, it is time to stop. Little or no good will result from pressing the argument. A great deal of good might be done by ceasing the argument. By ceasing you have demonstrated that you respect him as a person, and he may reciprocate by giving some thought to your points. In changing deep-seated attitudes the arousal of the defense of self should be avoided.

To change the strongly held attitudes of an individual one must gain first the respect and trust of that person. It is only by love that the self-defensive measures of the individual are prevented from arising. Through love you convince the individual that there is no necessity for defense.

Even love will not overcome the self-defenses of some persons. They may misconstrue your actions of love as aggressive and take defense measures.

CHANGING ATTITUDES THROUGH CHANGING GROUPS

If it is possible to remove an individual from a group and place him in a different group, attitudes may be affected. They will be affected to the extent that: (1) the attitudes of the groups are different; (2) the new group satisfies many of the needs of the individual; and (3) the members of the new group respect the individual and refrain from arousing self-defensive actions in him.

One of the purposes of inviting persons who are not active church members into a Sunday school is to provide a Christ-oriented group for them. We are seeking to take a person out of other groups and make him a member of a new group. In this Sunday school the new member communicates his feelings toward God and his fellow men. In order to communicate he must learn the attitudes and values of the group. This is a first step toward internalizing these attitudes and values. The person's original attitudes and values which conflict with those of the church group may be replaced because they are no longer rewarded. The new group member is not with former groups and does not communicate with them; thus the attitudes and values of the other groups are no longer rewarded or reinforced, and therefore, may be displaced. To provide a new environment is to provide new attitudes and values which are constantly reinforced by established group members.

This method is used in social work. Children may be sent to foster homes to provide a different group environment. The method is not likely to succeed if there is a lack of love for the person, or if the new group is weak.

CHANGING PERCEPTIONS

Self-defensive actions are aroused because we perceive a situation as threatening to us. We may interpret situations as threatening when in reality they do not threaten us. Sometimes strong defensive attitudes can be changed if the person learns to perceive a threatening situation as nonthreatening. We may learn through love that those we fear are willing to receive our love and that those we become aggressive toward are also in need. Our ego-defense is no longer necessary because we recognize others as having strengths and weaknesses just as we do.

Our Christian values must guide our approach to changing others' attitudes and values. We must *never* regard the information on how to change or maintain existing attitudes as "gimmicks" to change others against their will. God has given them the right to choose, and we must bear this in mind when we try to change them. To manipulate others is to regard them as objects rather than individuals and children of God.

SUPPLEMENTARY READINGS

These books will introduce the reader to a wider range of authors and theories in the field of personality and social psychology.

Douvan, Elizabeth, and Kaye, Carol. "Motivational Factors in College Entrance," *The American College*. Nevitt Sanford (ed.). New York: John Wiley and Sons, 1962.

Fromm, Erich. *Escape from Freedom*. New York: Holt, Rinehart & Winston, 1941.

Hiltner, Seward, and Menninger, Karl (eds.). *Constructive Aspects of Anxiety*. Nashville: Abingdon Press, 1963.

Miller, Daniel R., and Swanson, Guy E. *The Changing American Parent*. New York: John Wiley and Sons, 1958.

Newcomb, Theodore M. *The Acquaintance Process.* New York: Holt, Rinehart & Winston, 1961.

—————. *Social Psychology.* Rev. ed. New York: Holt, Rinehart & Winston, 1965.

—————. "Student Peer-Group Influence," *The American College.* Nevitt Sanford (ed.). New York: John Wiley and Sons, 1962.

Peck, Robert F., and Havighurst, Robert J. *The Psychology of Character Development.* New York: John Wiley and Sons, 1960.

Riesman, David. *The Lonely Crowd.* New Haven: Yale University Press, 1950.

Tillich, Paul. *The Courage to Be.* New Haven: Yale University Press, 1952.